ROCK STAR 101

A Rock Star's Guide to Survival and Success in the Music Business

by Marc Ferrari

ALLWORTH PRESS
NEW YORK

07 06 05 04 03 02   5 4 3 2 1

Published by Allworth Press
An imprint of Allworth Communications
10 East 23rd Street, New York, NY 10010

Cover design by Mary Belibasakis

Page composition/typography by SR Desktop Services, Ridge, NY

Library of Congress Cataloging-in-Publication Data
Ferrari, Marc.
Rock star 101: a rock star's guide to survival and success in the music business /
by Marc Ferrari.
p.   cm.
Includes bibliographical references (p.   ) and index.
ISBN 1-58115-227-2
1. Rock music—Vocational guidance.   2. Music trade.   I. Title: Rock star
one hundred one.   II. Title.
ML3795.F46   2002
781.66'023—dc21   2002000209

Printed in Canada

TABLE OF CONTENTS

DEDICATION

This book is dedicated to the memory of George Harrison,

whose extraordinary musical gifts and spirit of humanity have been an

unparalleled inspiration to me throughout my life.

ACKNOWLEDGMENTS

For my parents for their unconditional support to allow me to follow my dreams . . .

Many thanks to my bandmates in Keel, Cold Sweat, and Medicine Wheel . . . it's been a great ride. To all the bands/artists I mentioned in this book for your inspiration and dedication to the craft. To Mike Varney for The Big Break. To Tim Collins for the invaluable insights. To Dana Tomarken at NARAS for her help with *MusiCares.* To Randy Poe, John Braheny, Jai Josefs, Mark Abbattista, Henry Root, Ronnie Schiff, Barry Kolsky, Aaron Fischer, Hernando Courtright, Ken Cassidy, David Grossman, Linda Springer, Paul Hrisko, Ridge Walker, Todd Brabec, and Jeff Brabec for their assistance. To my brother Gary, Jeff Costell, and my angel Lorraine for being there for me.

And special thanks to Jodi Summers for making the phone call.

PREFACE
On the Road to Stardom: Steps and Stumbles

It's been said that music calms the savage beast. Truer words may
have never been spoken, especially in my case. I remember being
exposed to music at a very early age, as my parents were always
playing the radio or their favorite records on their hi-fi stereo system. Popular sounds of the day became imbedded in my memory,
such as my mom's favorites—Frank Sinatra, Jerry Vale, and the
Motown standards. Whenever a favorite song of mine would
come over the airwaves, I would stop what I was doing and just
absorb it—I became totally captivated. I didn't know why music
had this effect on me—it just did. I was drawn to it, and I didn't
question it.

Humans by nature *need* to express themselves—some by dance,
some by sport, some by spoken word, others by written word, some
by several of these, others by just one. The very moment in time
when a form of expression reveals itself to you as a natural path is
what I call a *power point*. There may be several of these power
points in your life, but everyone has at least one. It may be that
instant when the paintbrush you were holding seemed to draw by
itself, or perhaps you were practicing your ballet lessons and suddenly felt like you were being guided by something you could just
feel. Some people have a *level 2 power point* in their life, in which
they know in a specific instant that they want to dedicate their life
to their chosen form of expression. Dedicating one's life to a craft
usually entails trying to make a living at it. Unless you are independently wealthy or have other means to support yourself, this is the
dreaded moment where "commercialization" usually enters the picture. It is at this crucial juncture that the artist must try to maintain
the balance between being true to himself (i.e., "staying pure") and
using his talents and abilities to facilitate the financial survival that

will enable him to continue to develop that craft. It is indeed a tightrope that one must walk with the most delicate of balance.

My first power point occurred when I was eight and a half years old, but I remember it like it happened ten minutes ago: It has remained one of the most distinct moments of my life. We were visiting some cousins of mine, and I was being my usual rambunctious self, flying around the house a mile a minute, never giving my parents a moment of peace to catch up with the relatives. As I turned the corner to the living room, I noticed something on the couch—a guitar. Just a cheap, beat-up old acoustic with nylon strings. It was the most stunning sight I had ever seen. I went over to pick it up, as if it had asked me to do it. I can only compare it to the scene in *Close Encounters,* where Richard Dreyfuss sees the spaceship for the first time—as if it were predestined to happen, and you knew you already had experienced the moment.

I began strumming the guitar, awkwardly trying to coax some sounds out of it. It totally enthralled me, spoke to me, accepted me. My mom, noticing that there wasn't a shrieking eight-and-a-half-year-old terrorizing the house anymore, thought I may have knocked myself out by running into something (a feat I had managed to do several times before, with scars to prove it!). Instead, when she saw me holding the instrument, she came over and sat down next to me. We looked at each other and both *knew.* Not saying a word, she just smiled and gave me a kiss, then walked away. At that moment, I knew I had made an amazing discovery. My mom was relieved that I wasn't yelling or screaming, and I had found something that allowed me to make noise of another kind. I had experienced my first power point, and I would continue to make noise from that day forward.

For my ninth birthday in late January 1971, my parents bought me the same guitar that my cousin had. It was a $25 Stella acoustic, which I still have to this day. I remember waking up with it many a morning, having played myself to sleep. I enrolled at the local music store for weekly guitar lessons, learning the fundamentals of the instrument and how to read music.

In August 1971 my family moved to a small town near Rochester, New York. I quickly started lessons again at the local store, playing every moment I had a chance. Around that time I had seen the Beatles' movie *Let it Be,* and of course I just had to have an electric guitar like the one George Harrison and John Lennon used. It just so happened that the local music store had this red Guild Starfire electric guitar that was an exact replica of the more expensive Gretsch models that the Beatles were using. Problem was that it was $200. My parents gently informed me that they could not afford it on the money they were making at the time.

So, that summer, I set a goal for myself to get that $200 by my next birthday: I would just have to buy it for myself. I put a deposit of $20 on the Guild, and for the next six months or so I did anything I could to earn money, even if it was just a quarter at a time. I got a paper route. In the fall, I raked leaves. In the winter, I shoveled driveways. I carried groceries, walked dogs, and even watered plants for neighbors who were on vacation. By the time late January rolled around, I had saved up nearly the entire amount. With a little help from my grandfather as a birthday present, I finally had enough for the prized purchase. With that bright red Guild electric as my weapon of choice, there'd be no stopping this ten-year-old now! Of course, an amplifier was in order next, so the saving process began again immediately!

Much to their credit, my parents were largely responsible for nurturing in me a love for various types of music. We were always going to see concerts together, since there was a community college in our town that regularly featured national acts, and we were but an hour's drive from the bigger cities of Rochester and Buffalo. Before the age of thirteen, I had attended concerts by artists as diverse as jazz guitarist Charlie Byrd, José Feliciano, classical Maestro Andres Segovia, blues great B. B. King, and folk artists Tom Chapin, Gordon Lightfoot, and Don McLean, among others. This exposure to a variety of musical styles greatly expanded my musical horizons, and offered a wider palette of knowledge to absorb from; I feel that I became a more complete musician and person as a result.

I continued my love affair with the instrument, eventually becoming active in school plays and regional theater productions. In the sixth grade, I even put a band together, which played Beatles covers. We performed in the school talent show and put on our own miniconcert, complete with accompanying female "mania"!

Graduating to the seventh grade exposed me to the older, high school musicians who were more experienced and knowledgeable than I. I viewed this as a great opportunity to learn and absorb from their experience.

The guitarist in the school's most popular band was aware of who I was and took me under his wing. I became something of a musical disciple—watching, listening, absorbing, emulating. I went to as many band rehearsals as I could, wanting to see firsthand how a "real" band operated. I accompanied the band to various gigs they had around the area, such as weddings, graduation parties, school dances, 4-H events—you name it. It was all invaluable firsthand experience that I so desperately craved.

This was my first exposure to contemporary rock music, and I borrowed as many records as possible, each one opening up musical jewels like a new treasure that I had just unearthed. Bands such as Led Zeppelin, Bad Company, REO Speedwagon, the Outlaws, and Lynyrd Skynyrd were among the first bands that I listened to, and it's safe to say that they left their indelible imprint on me. About a year later, I was to experience my second power point.

The year 1976 was a great year for rock music. Maybe the bicentennial added to the overall energy of things, but for whatever reason, 1976 seemed to bring out the best in bands. The Eagles' *Hotel California*, Aerosmith's *Rocks* (far and away my favorite album of all time), Led Zeppelin's *Presence*, the first Pat Travers release, Thin Lizzy's *Jailbreak*, Peter Frampton's *Comes Alive*, Rush's *2112*, Ted Nugent's *Free for All*, Kansas' *Leftoverture*, Johnny Winter's *Captured Live*, Bad Company's *Run With the Pack*, Nazareth's classic *Hair of the Dog*, the first release from Starz, and Z.Z. Top's *Tejas* were among the releases of that year. Many of these releases are still selling well over twenty-five years later and are considered the apex of many of these bands' careers.

But as many albums as either Frampton or the Eagles may have sold that year, 1976 belonged to another band that ruled over the youth in a way that had never been seen, and hasn't been seen since. This band led an army of loyal followers who purchased records, concert tickets, and merchandise in record-breaking numbers, and influenced more hopeful rockers to pick up a guitar than anyone before. That year was owned by KISS—hands down. Their breakout single "Rock and Roll All Night" was a battle cry for a generation and flooded the airwaves starting early that year. I distinctly remember the first time I heard it: It was like a clarion call, awakening a sleeping animal inside of me. And even though I was hearing it on a tiny transistor radio, the energy of the song was captivating, drawing me into the fray, inviting me to the party.

The band announced a concert at the Niagara Falls Convention Center on April 14, 1976. Nothing short of a nuclear war would have prevented me from going. I persuaded some older kids from my neighborhood to take me and counted the days until the show. The wait seemed like an eternity, the anticipation gripping me like a vice. Even the one-hour ride to Niagara Falls felt like a lifetime—I couldn't get there soon enough. Pulling up to the parking area, my adrenaline started to flow as I saw hundreds upon hundreds of KISS fans streaming toward the front, bedecked in full makeup and custom-made jackets. As I entered the venue, I was suddenly overcome by the enormity of ten thousand gathered together in one mass of energy. I had never been in a building of that size, nor had I ever seen that many people in one place. If you could have tapped into the electricity in the air, it would have powered the world. It was like every single person's life force was wired together as one. When the lights went down, the ensuing roar of the 10,000 rock-starved denizens was the most powerful, primal, supercharged resonance this fourteen-year-old had ever heard. It was the call of the wild, and it was answered by the onslaught of the band as the opening notes crashed into sight and sound. And at the very millisecond that the band hit the stage, the 50,000 watts of power crashed into my chest, and the flash bombs and light towers assaulted my eyes, I *knew*—*more* than completely, 1,000 percent, unequivocally, undeniably, unquestionably—that the *only* thing I wanted to do in life was to be on that stage, too. Everything was so clear to me: In that very instant I had a goal, a vision, a quest. I didn't know *how* I was going to do it, but I knew *what* I was going to do, and many times in life, knowing *what* to do is more important. That second power point was even more dynamic and revealing than the first. The concert left me emotionally and physically drained, but at the same time charged with a purpose in life. From that moment on, I had a target to shoot for, a finish line to strive for. I wanted to be in a band on a major label, playing in major arenas and causing major havoc, just like KISS. It

was what I would devote my life to, and do just about anything to
obtain.

In late 1976 I went on to form my first professional band,
called Whiplash. The three other musicians were all seniors or had
graduated—all of them were a good four or five years older than
me—but I was the leader. I organized rehearsals (usually in my
parents' garage or cellar), arranged the songs, became the band's
manager, and even booked our shows—pretty tenacious for a kid
not even fifteen years old. We rehearsed three to four times a week,
covering a lot of Ted Nugent, Lynyrd Skynyrd, BTO, Aerosmith,
and, of course, KISS. We needed a P.A. system, so we all rigged up
some cabinets with junk speakers; my Dad just *loved* to lug those
around in the back of our family station wagon. A little sparse on
gear, our vocal mic was plugged in along with my guitar into the
same amp. We may have been naïve, but we all had a profound
love for the music we were playing, and it was always fun—an element that would be sorely missing in some future bands that I
would be involved with.

We played our first show in the spring of 1977 at a local
campground. Everything that could go wrong did. The P.A. quit
on us, an amp went, and strings were broken midsong, but we still
made it through and the owner asked us back. Our big pay? One
hundred dollars—we'd spent more than that on munchies for all
the rehearsals, but we were happy to know we were on our way. It
was a step in the right direction. Whiplash broke up in the fall of
'77, as some of the members moved out of town. I joined another
band in the spring of '78 called Southbound. We became one of
the best-drawing bands in the Western New York region, playing
to packed houses every weekend, and even coheadlining a few outdoor festivals. Those were some of the best times in my musical
career—playing for the sheer love of it, and developing a loyal following in the process. We even had our own fan club—a contingent
of a dozen or so girls with homemade Southbound T-shirts who
would come to every show within a seventy-five-mile radius. It was
the first time I realized the importance of having fans and what
they can do for the morale of a band. I stayed with Southbound
until I graduated from high school in January 1980.

In spite of my rock 'n' roll lifestyle of keeping late and long
hours rehearsing and traveling, I managed to graduate as the salu-

tatorian of my class with a 96.5 grade point average. I'd won a four-year Regents scholarship that I could have used for any state college in New York, but I didn't want to go back to school quite yet. I decided to put the scholarship on hold for a semester and follow my instincts. Later that summer, I attended a Judas Priest concert in Rochester and met a bunch of musicians from the Boston area who were following the band around. They were in the process of putting the "ultimate metal band" together, and they proceeded to fill my head with visions of how great the Boston music scene was.

So, in December 1980, I packed all my clothes and gear in a U-Haul, and with $500 and a bag of dreams, I set off for Beantown. The four-hundred-mile drive gave me a lot of time to think about the giant step I had just made. I was diving off the deep end without really knowing where the water was. Would I be able to support myself on my own? Would I be able to fit into a band with four new musicians? (I barely knew their names, never mind their playing styles!) Would we be able to establish the band within the highly competitive Boston area? Would I kill myself with my own cooking? These were all questions that were floating around my mind like a stubborn fly that I couldn't catch.

The first few weeks were trying, to say the least. It was the dead of winter, and the brutally cold New England wind was a solemn wake-up call. I initially slept on a couch in the band's rehearsal room until arrangements could be made for me to stay with a friend of the band. That wasn't much better—sleeping on the floor along with four high school dropouts whose only aim in life was to get high and watch *Star Trek* reruns. I knew my $500 wasn't going to last too long, so, for $3.50 an hour and a free lunch, I took a job at a restaurant bussing tables, washing dishes, and cleaning toilets. I began my daily chores at 6:30 A.M., busted my butt nonstop through the busy lunch hour, and by the time 3:30 P.M. rolled around, I was exhausted. To make things worse, I had an allergic reaction to the industrial-strength detergent used in the dishwasher. My hands became irritated at first, then my skin began to crack and bleed. After a while it affected my dexterity and playing, but I stuck it out because of my financial situation. We would usually rehearse until midnight, and by the time I got home I was looking at about five hours of sleep per night.

This lasted a few months until finally I realized that my career as a guitarist was more important than my career as a restaurant hack. I found another job that was more suited to the lifestyle of a musician: selling subscriptions to the local newspaper over the phone (a little more on rock 'n' roll jobs later on). A funny incident occurred around this time: Having little money for food, I was always looking for economical ways to eat. Almost every starving artist has gone through his Top Ramen or macaroni and cheese phase. I went through a Snickers phase. Well, it wasn't a long phase, but it had a lasting impact on me. A local supermarket was having a sale on Snickers—eight for a dollar. I was living on about $25 a week food money at that time, so I figured this would be an opportunity to invest in some inexpensive sustenance. I bought $10 worth and proceeded to live off those damn things for the next three weeks. By the end of the supply, I was on such a sugar rush that I was nearly seeing double. I haven't had one since—nearly twenty-one years later! A few years later, when Keel was interviewed for the national rock magazine *Hit Parader*, this story was featured as part of a "Food Stories of the Stars" series.

Slowly, things did get better for me gastronomically and economically. I eventually got my own place, met a girl, and moved in with her. High aspirations for our band, however, took a turn for the worse—by the time the fall rolled around, the band called it quits. Although the band hadn't set the world on fire, I'd learned a lot about promotion and showmanship, and would apply some of these principles to my later bands. I wasn't about to move back to Western New York, so I decided to stick it out and forge ahead. I enrolled at a music college and brushed up on my theory and technique. I got a job teaching guitar lessons at the local store in addition to my phone gig, making some decent money for a change—decent meaning about $200 per week—hardly wealth-building income! I was able to get some session work from an ad I placed in a local music magazine, and I even did a few sessions with ex-Rolling Stones producer Jimmy Miller. It was the first time that I had been involved with someone "famous," and the sessions gave me a little hope, helping to temporarily soothe my increasing frustrations.

There was a period in early '82 when I became depressed about the lack of progress in my career, and I began getting migraines. I knew what I *wanted* so badly, but I felt I wasn't get-ting any closer to making that a reality. I was jealous of the success of some of the other bands that were my age, particularly Def Leppard, and I just drove myself harder to try to match them. The migraines were so intense that there were times I was incapacitated. I thought for sure that I would have a brain hemorrhage. Sometimes, they lasted all day, and all I wanted to do was sleep or drink. I got a prescription for Valium and nearly became addicted to it. Of course, I was only solving one problem by creating another, and I was lucky I didn't become hooked or have an overdose. I hated the fact that I felt like I *needed* this drug to function. I had never been dependent on anything (or anyone) before, and I wasn't about to let it happen now. I bought a few books about positive thinking, and they helped me put things in a better perspective. The headaches eventually subsided, and I began to accept things for the way they were, letting things happen at their own pace. I joined a cover band in the summer of '82 just so I could keep my chops up, but I knew in my heart I was never going to make it playing some-one else's material.

In the summer of '83, there was a musical revolution starting to brew that would change my life forever. Heavy metal was finally beginning to catch on with the masses. It first started with British bands like Judas Priest, Def Leppard, Saxon, Motörhead, Iron Maiden, Ozzy Osbourne, and Whitesnake. Then, the American companies began signing bands as well. Twisted Sister, Riot, and the Rods (all from New York) started making noise. Los Angeles countered with bands such as Ratt, Mötley Crüe, Dokken, and Great White. All of these bands had independent releases in 1983. Then, Quiet Riot broke out in a huge way with the success of their album *Metal Health*, which sold over 5 million copies in the United States alone and catapulted them to superstardom. Adding fuel to the fire was the "US Festival" in the summer of 1983 that included a heavy metal day headlined by Van Halen and supported by Mötley Crüe, Quiet Riot, Triumph, Judas Priest, and others. Suddenly, heavy metal was the flavor of the month, and record companies scrambled to find the next big thing.

In September 1983, two bandmates from my cover band went to L.A. on vacation. They came back ranting and raving about how great everything was—the music, the beaches, the clubs, you name it. They even met two sisters at a club, went on a date, and both fell in love. We were pretty tired of playing the same Boston area clubs over and over again for no musical gratification, so we all decided that we would move out to California and re-form there. I had a hunch that L.A. was the place to be. All my favorite new bands were coming from there, the Olympics were coming in '84, which would focus a lot of attention on the city, and besides, if I was going to be starving, I might as well be starving in the sun, alongside the most beautiful girls in the world! After twenty-one years on the East Coast, I had had enough of six-month winters, anyway. My two lovestruck buddies couldn't get there soon enough, so we finished up our last commitment of shows the following month, and they left the next day. Our second guitarist (who was barely eighteen at the time) went with them, but our drummer didn't make the move out, as he was married and a bit older than us. I had made a promise to see my folks over the holidays, so I agreed to join my buddies in L.A. during the first week of January. The game plan was to find a drummer, get the band playing in Los Angeles, and become the "next big thing."

January 4, 1984, was the day. I boarded a 747 at Boston's Logan Airport and made a vow to myself that I wouldn't come back unless I had a record deal. When the plane entered the L.A. basin, I became almost paralyzed by the sight of the great expanse of lights beneath me. I had never seen a city that spread out like L.A.—almost one hundred miles in each direction. I remember thinking I would become lost in the maze and never find my way around this amazing spread of humanity. Here I was, moving lock, stock, and barrel again—taking another giant step. Never thinking twice about looking behind, just forging forward. So far, my gut instincts had served me wisely, and I had a great feeling about this move.

My three buds met me at the airport and proceeded to take me up to the famous "Sunset Strip," a section of Sunset Boulevard in West Hollywood which was home to some of the rock world's most famous nightclubs. In a particular quarter-mile section was the Whiskey, the Roxy, the Central, Gazzari's (where Van Halen once ruled), and the crown jewel hangout, the Rainbow. These clubs have played host to some of the most popular bands of all time. Several classic live albums have been recorded at the Roxy, and the Whiskey is well known as the site of Led Zeppelin's first Los

Angeles shows, playing a five-night stint opening up for Alice
Cooper in January 1969. My jaw dropped when I saw the streets
packed with long-haired rockers cruising the strip both by car and
on foot. Everywhere I looked, there was spandex, leather, chains,
boots, whips, handcuffs, hairspray, fishnets, headbands, earrings,
tattoos, makeup, glitter, sparkle. Guys, girls, straights, gays, bis,
trans, wealthy, homeless, ugly, gorgeous, dogs, cats, devils, and
angels. *Everything.* It was simply stunning—like being thrown into
a big, boiling cauldron and trying not to drown in the stew. I didn't
know if I was in America or in Oz—all I knew was that nothing in
my wildest dreams had prepared me for that moment. I loved it.

I was taken into the Rainbow, not knowing what I was in for.
The crowd inside was the same mix as the one outside. It was like
being in a circus, with hordes of performers swirling around and
mingling about. A little history about the place: It's been open in
various forms since the 1960s and is something of a cultural land-
mark. In the '70s, many of the maverick British bands such as Led
Zeppelin, the Who, and Deep Purple made it their club of choice
for partying and general debauchery. Many a lurid tale has been told
about goings-on under tables, in bathrooms, or in private booths
upstairs, but that's for another book altogether!

In the early evening, the Rainbow (which is actually an award-
winning Italian restaurant) draws an older dinner crowd. But by
10:00 P.M. the rockers take over, and the entire crowd is packed
into the joint like sardines. One can barely move in the aisles.
Dinner tables become parties unto themselves. Revelers spend the
entire evening hopping from table to table, circulating around its
horseshoe-shaped interior. Rock music blares over its arena-style
P.A. system, drowning out any chance of intimate conversation and
adding to the carnival-like atmosphere. The walls are bedecked
with various rock 'n' roll mementos such as guitars, photos, signed
albums, drums, and vintage posters, all testaments to the bands
who have made it such a famous spot. It was like Halloween, New
Year's Eve, and Mardi Gras thrown into a blender and turned to
ten—*every* night.

So, there I was, not one hour off the plane, green as can be,
being tossed into the "devil's den." I wound up at a table and the
drinks began to flow. During the course of the evening, various
acquaintances of my friends would come over, inquiring about "the

new kid." One of these acquaintances was a gorgeous little brunette named Nancy, who sat herself down next to me and proceeded to introduce herself. We spent the next few hours talking and laughing. I had made a friend. She couldn't believe that I had just moved here and had never been to the Rainbow before. I had a certain innocence that appealed to her, I guess. (L.A. hadn't corrupted me yet!) It turns out Nancy was a limo driver who had just finished work and had her car outside. She offered to take me up to Mulholland Drive to see the lights of the city. I'd never been in a limo before, and besides, I'd have been crazy to turn down an offer from a beautiful girl like that.

She took me up Laurel Canyon Boulevard to Mulholland, and we found a parking spot to watch the lights. The lights of the valley looked like diamonds, just within my grasp. Nancy turned out to be an extremely "friendly" girl, making me feel *very* welcome in L.A., and if my first night in the City of Angels was any indication, I was going to like this town a *lot*. I had purchased a round-trip ticket, since it was cheaper than one-way. The next day, I listed the return ticket in the paper. I knew I wasn't going back.

The next few weeks were spent getting myself situated and adapted to my new environs. The other guitarist and I were sleeping on the floor of the two-bedroom apartment belonging to our bandmates' new girlfriends, and there was so much junk in the house you could hardly move. Even the cockroaches felt crowded! My friends hadn't found jobs, nor had they done anything to find us a drummer or write new songs. Partying at the Rainbow and other clubs was the priority of the day.

Within a week, however, I got a job (telephone sales again!) and found a studio apartment one street over, which the other guitarist shared with me. I got a few of the local music papers and started calling some drummers, all the while trying to motivate the others to get things going. I was trying to juggle my job, my acclimation to the new area, my creative muse, and the band business all at the same time. Several weeks later, things had not moved forward that much on the band front, and I was not getting any help from the others. Tempers were beginning to fray.

One day, the guys called me to come over for a band meeting. I wasn't prepared for the bombshell they were to drop on me: The three of them were going to move back to Massachusetts! They gave me the excuse that their money had run out, their relationships with the girls had soured, and they had missed their families over the holidays. "Fine," I said. "Get a job, find another girlfriend, and go home for a visit. Simple solution." In spite of my efforts to convince them otherwise, they had their minds set and insisted they were going home for good. Needless to say, I was *devastated*. I had just uprooted my whole life, relocating to a strange city where I knew no one else. I had just taken the biggest leap of faith in my entire existence, placing all my belief and conviction in this new undertaking, not once entertaining the thought of returning to the East Coast. I had committed myself so entirely to this endeavor, not allowing the possibility of failure to enter the picture. And my friends were giving up the dream we had planned to share together just four short weeks after I had joined them. It really hurt. I felt abandoned, like I was stuck in a canoe with one oar. I didn't know what I was going to do.

That night, I went up to the Rainbow to drink alone. It was cold, and I brought along a leather jacket that had been a gift from my parents for my high school graduation. It had been with me since I'd left my hometown and had kept me warm through a lot of cold, lean times. This was the first time I had needed it in usually sunny Southern California. Once inside, I left the jacket at the table and proceeded to the restroom. When I returned not more than a minute later, the jacket was gone. It was like rubbing salt in an open wound. First, my friends announced they were abandoning me, now this. If bad luck strikes in threes, I didn't want to be around for the third one. Fortunately, I had my wallet with me, but it was still a quick, hard lesson about living in the city.

I tried to make some sense out of everything, but just couldn't. My hopes had been shattered and my resolve put to the test. I thought perhaps it was my fault this all had happened. My friends left shortly thereafter, and I spent the next few weeks trying to put it all behind me and move forward. I started to get depressed again, and the migraines returned. I put the word out that I was looking for a gig, but the world wasn't exactly knocking down a path to my door. Well, the word must have reached the right person upstairs, because fate was about to intervene.

It's been said that something good always comes out of something bad, just as every action has an equal and opposite reaction. I am a firm believer in this, as well as the concept of Karma. You can control your fate to a certain degree. There is also an element of destiny that is beyond any of our control. In my case, a little of both worked for me.

Since 1980, I had been in touch with a San Francisco–based music entrepreneur named Mike Varney. That year, he had started a small label called Shrapnel Records, which specialized in heavy metal. His goal was to discover and release the best unsigned heavy metal bands and solo artists in the United States. In a letter he wrote to *Guitar Player* magazine in early 1980, he announced his intentions to find the cream of the crop of U.S. talent and release his discoveries in a compilation called *U.S. Metal, Volume 1*. There had never been a label that specifically focused on this just-emerging genre of music. I answered the call, sending Mike a tape that I had made just before I left for Massachusetts. Although I didn't make the initial cut, Mike was impressed with my passion for and knowledge of hard rock music, and we became pen and phone pals. We would write each other about new bands we'd discovered or talk about the current releases from the bigger bands. We would pry each other for opinions and have long discussions about the state of the music industry in general. I turned him on to a world-class musician from the Western New York area named Billy Sheehan, who would later gain fame as bassist for David Lee Roth and Mr. Big. Mike would later write a new talent column for *Guitar Player* magazine, and featured Billy in one of the issues.

The month before my move to California, Mike had sent me a Christmas present of some albums he had just released on his label. The most intriguing one was a release by a band called Steeler, which featured Swedish guitar whiz Yngwie Malmsteen and a singer by the name of Ron Keel. The album was chock full of well-crafted rock anthems played with conviction, finesse, and superior musicianship. I called Mike just after Christmas to let him know I would be moving out to join some friends, and perhaps I would take a trip up to San Francisco to meet him after I got settled in.

Flash forward to L.A., 1984, when, as fate would have it, I was shopping for a jacket to replace the one that had just been stolen. I ran into Mike at a store on Melrose Avenue, and I recognized him right away, as his photo was in the *Guitar Player* magazine column. We had a rather exuberant exchange of hellos and how-the-hell-are-yous, and then I proceeded to tell him of my predicament of being alone in L.A. and in search of a band. Well, wouldn't you know it, Ron Keel was breaking up his band Steeler and going solo. Keel needed to find some musicians right away, since Mike was going to record and release this solo album on his label. Mike promised to talk to Ron on my behalf, and true to his word, he did. Ron called me the next day, and we got together to meet each other. Things clicked, and on Mike's recommendation, Ron hired me on the spot. The nucleus for Keel was born. The drummer from Steeler followed Ron into this new project, but everyone else was "fresh blood," the other two members having been friends of Ron's from Phoenix.

For the next six weeks, we would rehearse every single day of the week in a rundown warehouse that Ron rented on a monthly basis. Set in a gang territory area of South Los Angeles, the building was overrun with cockroaches and totally devoid of windows, becoming a sweaty steambath in the afternoon sun. It also doubled as living quarters for some of the guys and road crew. Our gear was set up in a small rectangular room that was no more than six feet from back to front, forcing us to play literally with our noses to the front wall. With the amps, drums, and P.A. system all blaring at the same time, the volume was deafening, shaking the walls. Rehearsal typically consisted of learning new songs, vocal exercises, working on choreography (big in those days), and then running the set list down over and over and over again in drill-camp military fashion. By the time our first show rolled around, we were like a musical army on tactical alert: tight as nails, polished, and ready for battle.

On April 7, 1984, we made our debut at Perkins Palace in Pasadena to a sold-out show of nearly two thousand rabid metal lovers. There was a big buzz on the band, which helped fuel the frenzy, and we did not disappoint. Hitting the stage for the first time in California was like vindication for everything I had gone through getting to this point. There was a certain electricity in the air, and I knew that this band was capable of doing anything. Coincidentally, the first band on the bill that night was Stryper, who would later go on to have several gold and platinum albums.

Momentum was building quickly. In June 1984, we recorded our debut album *Lay Down the Law* for Mike Varney's label. We were also featured on Mike Varney's *U.S. Metal Volume 4*. We consistently sold out various venues in L.A., such as the Roxy, the Troubadour (two-night stand sold out!), and the Country Club, and the record company types started coming around. Barely two months later, we signed our major-label deal with Goldmountain Records, distributed by A&M. Gene Simmons of KISS was called in to produce, and already some of the rock press were touting us as "the next big thing." We went into the studio later that month to record *The Right to Rock*, finishing the project in a scant three weeks. I had been in California less than eight months and had recorded not one, but two albums, achieving my lifelong dream of signing a major-label deal and recording with one of my musical idols. Things were happening so quickly, I hardly had a chance to think about it.

In January 1985, *The Right to Rock* was released, and my world as I knew it was forever changed. The accompanying video for the title track went on to become an MTV favorite, staying in heavy rotation for months. The song itself became a battle cry for the rock masses, as it spoke of the freedom to express oneself and of standing up to defend one's beliefs. In light of threats from the Tipper Gore–led bastion of the P.M.R.C. (the Parents' Music Resource Center), the timing couldn't have been better. The P.M.R.C. wanted rating controls on records and concerts, and its leaders were poised to use their political clout to see this happen. This was viewed as a threat to First Amendment rights and a challenge to the record industry in particular. Our song came to sum up the frustrations of our generation of rock-starved youth and was featured in many news programs of the day. The reviews of the album were overwhelmingly positive, and we became favorites of the press. It seemed we could do no wrong.

We toured for most of the year, pairing up with the Japanese band Loudness, the German band Accept, and Canadian rockers Helix (a true testament to the international appeal of rock!). We crisscrossed the country several times, covering nearly every major market. The dividends paid off handsomely. Keel was voted "best new band" by three of the nation's biggest rock magazines: *Circus*, *Metal Edge*, and *Rock Scene*, beating out bands such as Metallica, Bon Jovi, and Dokken in the process.

In the next two years we would release two more albums, *The Final Frontier* and *Keel*, as well as having a song on the soundtrack to the movie *Dudes*. We would go on to play nearly 450 shows in seventeen countries on three continents, playing with bands such as Queensrÿche, Dio, Quiet Riot, Krokus, Aerosmith, and others. We played the Texxas Jam with Van Halen in front of 80,000 people and were special guests to Bon Jovi on the *Slippery When Wet* tour, 1987's highest-grossing concert tour. We even did a show at the United Nations building, which was broadcast worldwide as part of a cultural exchange program promoting world peace. We filmed seven videos and sold upwards of 1.5 million records worldwide. Throughout it all, we were having a great time, seeing the world, experiencing new things, and making enough to get by.

Eventually, we all started to get a little frustrated with not making the kind of money we *thought* we would be making, while seeing some of our friends become millionaires. It was beginning to wear on us, as we were on the road nearly eight months out of every year and were coming home nearly broke. All in all, it was an amazing ride, like catching a great big wave and riding it all the way into shore. And while we were surfing that big wave, it was a hell of a feeling, to be sure. I never wanted it to end, but as with all good things, it always does.

In early 1988, things came to a head between me and a few of the other guys. I had certain opinions on how the band should adapt to some changing musical tastes. I also disagreed with the way our band business had been running up to that point and had some ideas on how to rectify some of our financial concerns. I didn't have much support from the other members, so instead of being a thorn in everyone's side, I decided it was best for me to leave and go out on my own. Leaving the security of a major-label contract was a huge gamble, as I was essentially starting all over again, and there was no guarantee that I would be picked up by another label. But I had faith and a belief in my abilities, and decided that it was a risk worth taking.

I formed another band immediately, and after just seven live shows, we were signed to MCA Records. The band changed names and lineups several times before deciding on the name Cold Sweat, taken from a Thin Lizzy song. After a few delays, we released an album called *Break Out* in June 1990. We toured for the bulk of the year, including a jaunt to Europe, where we opened up for Whitesnake at an outdoor festival with over 50,000 in attendance.

While we didn't exactly set any sales records, *Break Out* was a real solid effort, and one that I am still very proud of. I had proven to myself that I had what it took to make it on my own, and that my gut instincts had served me correctly once again.

Keel went on to record an album called *Larger Than Live*, which was half-live, half-studio, but it never recaptured the energy or excitement of earlier efforts. Although I didn't play on that record, I was represented in the form of several songs I'd written. Amazingly, several years later, I became the owner of that record, as I bought the rights to the recordings from the label. I then repackaged it with a European company and turned a tidy profit. Keel broke up shortly thereafter, and the guys all went on to separate projects. The back catalog continues to sell to this day, generating income for me every year.

Success is a journey, not a destination. It can lead to wealth or to poverty, to fame or to obscurity, to elation or to disappointment. Along my journey, I learned by firsthand experience, and sometimes by mistake. In this business, there's not a lot of room for mistakes, and a bad one can affect you the rest of your life. But how do you know about potential mistakes or pitfalls if you don't have a reference? How do you know where the bad sections of town are unless you know the town? There're no high school classes or college courses to prepare you for a career in rock 'n' roll. No diplomas or degrees awarded at the end of the day. No guaranteed salary, benefits, pensions, or job security. This book was written to be your textbook, to be your guide to avoiding some common (and sometimes career-ending) mistakes that so often plague inexperienced musicians. Read it. Absorb it. Learn from it.

Remember this: There is more business than music in the music business, and it is indeed a *business* with a capital *B*. Knowledge is golden: Let this book be your gold mine.

CHAPTER 1
The Game: What It's Really All About

One can equate a career in the music business with being a lion trainer. The music business can be a wild animal: mean, hungry, unforgiving, and capable of doing great damage to the unprepared at any given moment. Even the most experienced of trainers have to be on their guard at all times, for fear of losing their heads in the jaws of the beast. Sure, a trainer can tame the creature, getting it to do tricks or making it feign friendship, but beneath the façade is a ruthless, self-serving man-eater whose only thought is for its own survival. If you take the position of wanting to be a trainer to this game, you must know the risks going in. To minimize your potential for loss, you must understand the nature of the beast. You must know its tendencies and anticipate its every move. You must know where you stand in *its* relationship to *you*. You must fully be aware of any factor that may affect your outcome. The record industry has been known to chew up its victims and spit them out barely alive. You may escape, but most often you'll be demoralized, starved, or near artistic death. However, if you go into the cage armed for battle with every advantage that you can possibly have, you will have a better chance of escaping unscathed. Before jumping headfirst into the fray, however, ask yourself if you're really up to the task. A career in the entertainment industry can be extremely exciting and rewarding on many levels. Countless people dream about becoming rock stars, movie stars, or sports stars when they're young. However, in addition to a lot of hard work, sacrifice, and frugality, the path to an entertainment career is usually filled with uncertainties and disappointments. Not everyone is cut out for it, and those who don't have the stomach for repeated setbacks or failures may be better suited for a different career. We've all heard the stories about those who have gone as far as taking their own lives out of depression over repeated failures, so a little mental preparation may go a long way in helping you make your decision in moving forward.

While we're on the subject of preparation, I'd like to say a few words about one of the most important basics in a music career: reading music. You've heard the expression "reading is fundamental." Well, this applies to music as much as it does to the written word. While it's true that some of the greatest and most well-known musicians do not know how to read music, I strongly urge everyone to learn how to read and write, since it may help open some doors in the future—such as lucrative studio sessions, commercials, and film and TV work. (More on this later.) Long after your touring days are over, you can still have a well-paying career if you have the necessary skills—and reading is one of them.

The biggest beast in the kingdom of the music industry is the *record company*. It is to the music industry what the Tyrannosaurus Rex is to dinosaurs—the largest, meanest, angriest, most temperamental member of the family, capable of generating the choicest of rewards, but also capable of inflicting the most serious damage. There are dozens of so-called major labels in the industry, but ultimately, they are all owned by just five supercompanies: Vivendi-Universal, AOL Time Warner, EMI, BMG, and Sony. And even though the record industry started in the United States, only one of these supercompanies is now 100 percent American-owned: AOL Time Warner!

EMI is British, BMG is German, Sony is Japanese, and Vivendi-Universal is French. All of these companies have stockholders to report to on an annual basis, and the prime goal of any major-label president is to have a better bottom line than he did last year. A bigger bottom line equals bigger profit. It's simple math. Special perks, such as increased expense accounts, bonuses, and stock options, serve as incentives for those at the label who have key marketing or executive positions. Stripped down to its bare bones, the major-label record company is nothing more than a well-oiled moneymaking machine.

The main reason why *any* artist gets signed is that the company thinks it can make a profit. It is very easy for a huge, multinational conglomerate to lose sight of the social responsibility of finding, developing, and nurturing talented artists. Granted, there may be some smaller, independent labels that may have more of a real concern for the artists they sign and for the music they release, but even the smallest of labels are still motivated at least somewhat by the prospect of financial gain.

The record industry continues to grow year after year, the bottom line well into the billions. The bigger it grows, the more impersonal it becomes. I know of many artists who have met their company representatives just a few times in their career, and I know several artists who have *never* met their reps. Long gone are the days when record company reps would "discover" an artist, take the artist under their wing, find the material, go into the studio, oversee the recording and production processes, and get involved with the marketing. There are so many divisions in a record company, you'd think you were dealing with an army. For example, most companies have an *A&R* (artist and repertoire) staff, a promotion division, a marketing division, a press division, a video division, a royalty/accounting division, a radio division, and an outside sales force. Because of the complexity of today's companies, many times, one division doesn't know what another one is doing. Lack of communication between these divisions can be fatal to an artist's career.

Think of a successful record as a relay race. In a successful race, team members must take their lap around the track and hand the baton off to someone else, who must then shoulder the same responsibility. The band always takes the first lap around the track and turns in a record. The record (baton) is then passed onto the various divisions that must work in conjunction with each other to ensure that success. The individuals in each division take their lap around the track and so forth. It's a team effort. Yet too often in the record industry, the baton gets dropped. When the baton falls, at the very least, the momentum is severely impeded, and many times, the race is over.

The most fundamental common denominator in the music industry is music itself, although sometimes you wouldn't know it. The business aspects all too often overshadow the musical aspects. The very act of vocalizing or playing an instrument is an expression of human emotion, deep-rooted in the soul. It needs to surface, just like air bubbles from the bottom of the ocean. Whether it's the yearning for recognition, the desire for fame, or the quest for fortune, this driving motivation is indeed an indomitable force that is always fueled with passion. In the innocence of youth and in the untainted realm of a non–music-business environment, the sheer joy of musical expression is as close to communicating with the heavens as one can get. When your soul is stirring through your body and your chosen instrument becomes the channel through which your creative energies flow, you truly can become "one with the world." In instants like this, it is easy to become lost in the moment. We're not *lost*, of course; if anything, we've *joined* the moment.

You may have seen how Tibetan monks can achieve trancelike states by repetitive chanting or how African tribesmen can drum their way into altered states of consciousness. It's the power of the human soul using a musical medium to transfer energy. It's pure. It's intense. It's real. It's in our genetic makeup. Only when the element of commerce is thrown into the mix do we begin to lose the purity and intensity of this beautiful musical energy. The negative energies needed to attain and sustain the commercialization of musical expression have a diluting impact on this natural life force. Like a faucet tightening up, so that a once-powerful water flow is but a few drops, these negative energies weaken our natural creative output, sometimes to the point of permanent stoppage. Writer's block is the perfect example of how negative energies such as anxiety, stress, apprehension, or fear can dam even the swiftest of rivers. *Negative energy does not exist in a pure state.* One of the hardest challenges any creative person has to face is learning how to balance the pure artistic side with the exploitive commercial side. It can be done, but it takes some effort. How can you overcome these negative energies? Use your power points.

Earlier, I spoke of power points and how they can affect your life in a positive way. You will know when your power points occur; they will strike you as the most natural, instinctive, fundamental truths that you will ever know. They happen at different times and for different reasons from person to person, but they all act as a conduit to channel creative energies and converge them to a narrow focus. Think of your power point as a funnel. Funnels gather from a wide source—a little here and there, collecting from the fringes. The output is stronger, faster, and more concentrated than the input, yet it constitutes the same amount as the original input. Power points are like lights that go on in a darkroom, illuminating paths and showing you the way. Once you have established a goal, your subconscious starts working to achieve it.

A lot of people think that there is such a thing as an overnight success. I'm here to tell you that there has *never* been an "overnight" success any time in the whole *entertainment* industry, never mind the music industry. It is a fallacy perpetuated by myth and hype. Success is a journey, not a destination. Some take the journey farther than others. Some take longer than others. Sadly, some don't return from the journey. There are a lot of detours, pitfalls, and setbacks that can impede one's progress. If you know the road, you can avoid some of these. I've been on that road before, and I will be your rock 'n' roll tour guide. I'll point out the things that will make your journey a little less bumpy and a little more rewarding. I'll show you some shortcuts and steer you away from paths that may lead to harm. So buckle up and come along for the ride!

CHAPTER 2
Getting Started: Building the Buzz,
Preparing for Battle

My favorite time: On stage!
©1987 Neil Zlozower.

Getting a band started and off the ground is kind of like building a fire. Some people are better at it than others, and there are certainly several ways to light one. Sometimes the fire smolders for a while and never catches; other times, it rages, engulfing everything. Events attract attention. Attention begets curiosity. Curiosity begets desire. Desire begets action. Attention is a strange animal, as it perpetuates itself. If there is a crowd of people standing around watching something (say, for instance, a street performer), more people are attracted because of the *crowd,* not so much because of the performer. People, by nature, want to know *what* other people are interested in, and *why* they're interested. And the assumption is that *because* people are interested in something, it must be good. If an A&R rep sees other A&R reps at a show, he or she thinks that *they* must think there's something special about the band. "If someone else wants it, it must be good," is the line of thinking. This is how bidding wars are created. There have been many examples of bands that had no offers whatsoever, but as soon as one label made an offer, others jumped in at the same time. This snowball effect is one of the most important weapons a band can have in its early days. Getting to that point is another matter, and that is the focus of this chapter.

First off, talent and success don't always go hand in hand. And while it's true that some talented people have gotten signed and made a fortune, there are lots of talented people who never even get signed, never mind make a living. It's also true that there are a lot of marginally talented or untalented people who have made a fortune as well. Life isn't always fair, and we all have to accept that.

Let's assume that you have gotten a band together (or are going it solo) and have begun to write some original material. This is important, because record companies want to sign unique, individual talent, and writing your own material is an important part of that. I can't think of too many rock artists who have gotten a deal playing solely other people's material. It happens more often in other genres of music—country, R&B, and pop—where, traditionally, a lot of outside material is used, and it's the voice or persona of the artist that is the main selling point. In the rock arena, original material is the king. Finding the right band members who share your musical vision and with whom you can get along has always been one of the hardest parts in getting started. Sometimes, you don't know certain things about a person unless you've had some time to work together. It may be that you don't agree on more personal levels than musical ones, but you must approach a band situation like a marriage. You are entering into a bond with these people and you are blending your talents and influences into one unit. Granted, there are instances where there may be a star or front person of the group, but normally, at least in the beginning stages, there's a whole band working together trying to get the train running down the track. Breakups tend to be ugly, sticky affairs, both in personal and band relationships, so before you commit to each other, be sure you know it's the "right thing."

PARTNERSHIP AGREEMENTS

While we're on the subject of breakups, now is the time to bring up the sometimes uncomfortable subject of inter-band business arrangements. Getting certain things out of the way early on is essential to the stability of a band. Once difficult things are put behind everyone, the focus can be shifted to more creative, productive concerns. I believe it to be of utmost importance that band members have an arrangement between themselves that clearly spells out everyone's role in the band. This arrangement, called a *partnership agreement*, is a legally binding document that should be drafted by an attorney and signed by all parties. A partnership agreement is an all-encompassing contract which, among other things, defines everyone's relationship to each other, spells out responsibilities among the parties to each other and to the unit, and determines what financial interest each member will receive, and from which sources. The agreement may also outline such things as ownership of the name of the group, voluntary withdrawal of a member (and subsequent penalties), processes and causes for expulsion of a member, ownership of communal property such as endorsements, and repayment of debt that the partnership may owe to an individual partner. There is no "standard" partnership agreement—they are all tailored to each individual situation, since each band has a different set of circumstances.

DIVIDING THE MONEY

The issue of dividing up monies that may be generated has always been a matter of contention within bands. There are several major sources of income that are normally generated:

Artist Royalties.

These are paid by the record company to a designee for the sale of albums, cassettes, and CDs. This is based on the number of *points* that a band may receive on each album sold. Each point equals roughly 1 percent of the suggested retail price of the unit sold.

Publishing Royalties (a.k.a. Mechanical Income).

Also paid by the record company, publishing royalties go to the publishers and writers of each song on an album. The maximum amount of publishing income payable on each record sold is based on the *statutory mechanical rate* at the time of the album's release, which is currently eight cents per song and increases every two years. Most record companies will pay on a maximum of ten songs, but then pay only on 75 percent of the total, which is called *¾ rate*. Therefore, if a band wrote all ten songs on its album, it would earn an additional sixty cents per album in publishing income (10 × 8.0 × .75). Many times, bands who double as writers will take an advance on their future publishing income. Additional publishing income can come from sheet music or music folio sales, which can be a separate deal from the initial music publishing portion. This money can be divided in a number of different ways, some of which I'll outline a little later in this chapter.

Performance Income.

When songs are publicly performed or played on the radio or TV, a royalty is generated and paid to the writers and publishers of that song via a performance rights organization, or P.R.O. There are three major P.R.O.s in the United States: ASCAP, BMI, and SESAC. Their main function is to track these public performances, issue licenses to those entities that use them, and pay their writer and publisher affiliates their appropriate share. Domestic royalties are paid quarterly, and foreign royalties three or four times a year, depending on the society.

Merchandising Income.

Often the most lucrative aspect of the money train, merchandising income includes monies generated by the sale of T-shirts, tour program books, and other items that may carry the band name or logo. Very often, these monies can be more substantial than artist royalties, or even publishing income. Some bands may even have fan club revenue on top of merchandising income.

Touring Revenue.

These are monies that are available for disbursement if the band turns a profit on the road after paying all commissions, salaries, and tour expenses.

Getting the unpleasant business of finances out of the way early on will make for a happier, healthier band. However, prepare to do some battle among yourselves—it's never easy getting a number of people to agree about money.

There are several different schools of thought on the subject of splitting the profits. Some bands divide everything equally from all sources at all times. This certainly is the most democratic way and, at the same time, the most "communistic" way of doing things. This approach may certainly alleviate the element of jealousy between band members and also prevent ulterior motives from clouding a creative decision. For example, when publishing royalties go only to the songwriters in the band, those band members may favor the songs they've written over those they haven't. With an equal-split type of

arrangement, each band member should feel on an equal foot-
ing with the others, and therefore pull for the *team* more
enthusiastically.

Conversely, if a certain band member is not particularly
motivated by nature, this equal-split type of arrangement may
have the opposite effect, causing that member to feel, "Hey, I'm
going to make as much as Joe over here anyway. Let him make
all the phone calls and arrangements; I'm going to take the day
off." Some bands have conditions built into their partnerships to
prevent this kind of behavior. If someone keeps missing rehearsals or fails to perform certain duties, he may be penalized.

Other bands may decide to split up certain monies equally,
such as artist royalties and merchandising, while other income,
such as publishing royalties, may be split up in proportion to a
band member's actual involvement. Here are my personal
thoughts on the various income streams and how they should
be divided:

Artist Royalties

I feel artist royalties should be split equally among band members, provided that all members have been in the band the same
amount of time and have pulled their equal share of the weight.
However, if a band gets a new member just before it signs a
deal, and the new kid did not go through the torturous process
of getting the deal, then perhaps the new member should get a
reduced share of artist royalties on the first album but an equal
share on all subsequent ones. We will make the assumption that
all members of the band are signing the record deal in this case.
If the label decides to sign just the enigmatic lead singer or the
blistering-hot guitar player, this throws a whole other set of circumstances into the picture, creating a more complex scenario
in which an attorney's advice may be in order.

Merchandising and Tour Profits

As long as all band members are on the road together for the
same tour, there's no reason why monies related to the touring

shouldn't be split equally. Each member is on the stage or in the van the same amount of time as the others, spending the exact same amount of time on the overall tour. Regardless of how long a member may have been in the band up to this point, once on the road, everybody's time is equal and should be compensated as such.

Publishing Income

This is a big point of contention, since publishing income has the most long-lasting residual effect of any type of income. Long after a band has split up and merchandising income has vanished, long after the label drops you, leaving you hundreds of thousands of dollars unrecouped (with nary a dime in artist royalties ever made), publishing income can continue to pour in. Perhaps a song from the band is on a compilation album that is put out, or a whole album is repackaged by a company specializing in reissues. Or maybe a new band decides it likes your first single and decides to recut it for its own album. How about that major motion picture that just happens to need some background music for a bar scene, and the music supervisor happens to be a fan of yours? Bingo: residual *publishing* income.

I have always believed that songwriting is a craft. It is a skill that can be learned, honed, and perfected, but not everyone has the talent for it. There are talented writers, and there are *gifted* writers. While just about everyone is talented in some way, not everyone is gifted, and there is a big difference between the two. Not everyone is a writer, and, for this reason, I believe that writers should be justly compensated for their craft over and beyond what they may earn from other sources within the band. After all, this is the business of music, and the creators of the music have a right to benefit from their creations. At the same time, because publishing income makes up such an important portion of a band's overall income, the nonwriting members of a band should participate in this income as well. There are a number of creative scenarios that everyone can feel comfortable with:

Equal Split.

Some bands may choose to split up everything equally, either by having each band member be an equal-equity participant in a group publishing company or by assigning equal writer's share to each individual's own publishing company. Because of the volatility of rock bands, it's usually easier if each member has his *own* company. That way, if a member leaves (or is asked to leave), it would be easier to separate the departing member's account from the rest of the group. Penalties may be incorporated that would deduct a certain percentage if the band member were to leave in the middle of a tour or other inopportune time.

Token Split.

Each member would be entitled to a token portion of each song, regardless of his actual participation.

Nonwriting Participation.

All members would be guaranteed a certain percentage of the overall publishing income, even if their names were not listed as writers.

Full Speed Ahead . . .

Once this hurdle of compensation has been cleared, it should provide much smoother sailing for everyone as a whole. Unfortunately, hammering out a partnership agreement can be a painful process, but it is necessary. When this agreement is in place, it's time to move forward and sign that record deal that will hopefully generate all those dollars you just agreed to split up in a (presumably) fair manner! Figure 2.1 illustrates how various types of income are generated and how they are typically affected by commissions, splits, and taxes.

FIGURE 2.1. *Income and outflow for a band's finances.*

HOW TO GET YOUR RECORDING SESSION

The next order of business should be to record some material and start the "fire-building" process I mentioned earlier. Like computers, recording equipment gets better and costs less every year. It is possible to buy a digital recorder, a mixing board, and some signal-processing equipment for less than you'd pay for renting a studio in some cases. Granted, not everyone has the ability to afford that kind of expense, but if you are going to borrow money or take out a loan for a studio session, you might as well own the gear; you can always sell it later if the band breaks up.

Almost every musician knows at least one person who has some kind of recording gear, and almost every major city has *some* kind of studio. Short of borrowing money from parents, siblings, friends, sugar mamas and daddies, or loan sharks, there are still some resourceful ways you may be able to get that recording done, which may involve little or no monetary outlay.

Local Schools

Many junior highs, senior highs, and local colleges have either an audiovisual sciences department or a recording science program. Ask the instructor if there are any class projects that need a band for guinea pig purposes. While you're at it, see if there is a video or film program as well—you may get a free video out of it, too. This approach works for Internet Web sites as well. Almost every computer nerd is a closet Web site designer.

Spec Time at Studios

There's nothing worse for a recording studio than *downtime*—periods of inactivity when the studio doesn't have clients. When studios do not have paying clients, they are losing money by the hour. Oftentimes, studios will give bands what's known as *spec time,* whereby they will let a band record "free" (or for a nominal charge, writing the spec time off as a tax loss) in exchange for compensation at a later date. This compensation may be a

repayment of the actual rental fee the studio would have
received under normal booking rates, or it may constitute a
percentage of a record deal that may be derived from the
spec recordings.

Local Advertising Agencies and Radio Stations

Ad agencies often look for inexpensive means to promote their
clients. Many of these agencies have their own studios, and they
may agree to let you record some of your original material if you
create a song for them as barter. Local radio stations sometimes
create these ads as well, and they, too, may consider offering
studio time to your band in exchange for your musical services.

Local Clubs

Most local clubs have at least a decent P.A. system and some
kind of recording deck. If you are playing live, you can always
tape your performance; however, you may not have the ability to
re-record over mistakes. Perhaps the club would allow you to
record when it is closed. It's to the club's benefit that the band
has tapes that generate public interest, bringing patrons through
the doors.

Local Talent Scouts and Producers

If you live in an area that has a burgeoning music scene, chances
are there are local musicians and producers who get involved
with up-and-coming bands or individual artists. Everyone wants
to be the person who discovers the "next big thing." Usually,
there is a price attached to this, such as a commission or an
involvement with future record deals. The producer may ask you
to sign a *production deal* with him. With a typical production
deal, you are signing to the producer as an artist, who then in
turn will try to sign his deal with you to the record company. In
this type of arrangement, you wouldn't be signing to the record
company directly, but through the production deal you have
with the producer. Try to avoid this type of arrangement, if possible, as it puts you in less of a bargaining position with the

label for future negotiations. Most labels would prefer to negotiate with an artist directly, and you don't want to run the risk of
a third party, such as a producer, blowing a perfectly good deal
if he's too greedy. He may alienate a label if he makes unrealistic
demands to feather his own nest. If the producer insists on a
percentage of your deal and he helped earn it, fine. But don't
enter into a production deal arrangement with him unless there
are provisions that enable you to sign directly to the label.

CASSETTE AND CD ETIQUETTE

Okay, you've cajoled some of the above resources into recording
your demo. You've poured your heart and soul into the recording, and you're proud of the results. Hopefully, you were able to
track half a dozen or so songs for now. There's no logic in having a great quantity of mediocre songs—it's much better to
concentrate on making great quality, not quantity. Pick your
best three and sequence them so that the strongest song is
first. As far as technical aspects go, make sure to use Chrome
tape (high position CR02), which is the highest-grade tape.
Too many bands make the mistake of spending time, money,
and effort on creating what could be a great musical statement, then cut corners in the last step of the process by using
inferior grade Type 1, normal position tapes. Spend the extra
dollar for the best possible sound reproduction from your
source tape. Insist on having the cassettes done at *real time,*
as opposed to high-speed duplication, and leave off the
Dolby noise reduction; not everybody has that option on
their stereo systems.

If you have the financial resources to do a mass-pressing of
CDs, that's great, but you might as well wait until you have
enough material for an entire album, as the cost may be prohib-
itive. Minimum pressing for CD replication is typically 500
units, and package deals start at about $1,000. Normally, you
have to provide the plant with artwork in the form of film com-
posites, which can run into the thousands as well. If you have a
CD burner, you can burn individual CDs, since blank CDs have

come down in price to about twenty cents apiece. If you're planning on pressing more than a couple hundred pieces, you'd be better off going with a package deal, strictly from the viewpoint of saving time and wear and tear on the CD burner.

Once you have your product in hand, it's time to start creating a buzz for your band and getting your music heard by the right people.

BREAKING DOWN THE DOORS TO THE MUSIC BUSINESS

Getting your music to the right people can sometimes be a challenge, owing to the "closed-door" policies held by many record labels and publishing companies. Major label companies will not accept unsolicited material for two main reasons: First off, the volume of tapes would be overwhelming, and they could not possibly listen to everything that came in; and second, writers have tried to make claims against companies that have accepted unsolicited material in the past, insisting their material has been stolen or passed off to another of the label's artists.

Record companies meticulously log every tape that comes in. They monitor who requested it, which staff member received it, and the status of every submission. This way, if an unknown writer or artist tries to sue the label because he thinks the company gave his tape to a superstar, the label can track the history of that tape.

Don't even think about trying to hand-deliver a tape to a label. They all have heavy security, and you won't even get to the front door in some cases. Given the Fort Knox–type atmosphere at some of these labels, you may be wondering, "How do I break in?" Well, there are some tried and true means to crack the safe. And remember: If you're *that good,* they'll find *you.* All the labels have their antennae out, trying to beat their competitors to find and sign the best new talent. The following are some avenues to explore in getting your tape out and heard by as many different industry types as possible.

Attorneys

More and more, attorneys are acting as conduits to the labels.
Attorneys deal with labels on a daily basis. They represent
artists who are signed to the label or help broker licensing deals
with the label. Some act as independent counsel to the labels in
civil suits or other litigation. They already have a working relationship with the label, and they know the A&R staff very well.
There are some attorneys who specialize in getting bands deals.
It is a common practice for them to ask for a *retainer*, a fee to
help them offset their costs before they will *shop* (represent)
your tape. They may also ask for a percentage of a deal they may
get for you, whether it be in the form of a percentage of your
advance or a cut of the royalty points on your album.

I have conflicting thoughts on retainer agreements. I think
that if someone truly believes in you, he wouldn't (or shouldn't)
ask for a retainer—that's money that has to come out of your
pocket now, remember. Rather, he would take these expenses
only if he gets you a deal. If your attorney is worth his salt, he
may be able to negotiate additional points or a higher advance
from the record company, and take his commissions out of that,
essentially providing his services for free. I have heard of situations in which the attorney actually made out better than the
client. If the band has four or five members in it, by the time
things get split up, it's entirely possible that this can happen. I
also understand that attorneys have to make a living as well, and
they can't spend an abundance of their high-priced billing time
on speculative deals, which is the reason that many of them ask
for retainers in the first place.

Managers

Managers have a vested interest in your career: They benefit if
you get a record deal. But when is the best time to seek a management deal? There are those who feel that if you can go it
alone and secure a record deal by yourself, you could conceivably
hire a manager much later in the game. That way, the manager
wouldn't commission certain monies, such as your record

advance or publishing deal, because, presumably, you already had one in place. Theoretically, you would be saving money on some commissions under this scenario. However, don't be "penny-wise but dollar-dumber" in your thinking. In the early stages, a manager can be an extremely important asset. Many managers have long-standing relationships with labels, and they can get decision makers on the phone. They may even act as investors, paying for demos, photo sessions, press kits, rehearsals, clothes, and so on. Many times, managers are the *only* ones who believe in your talent when everyone else is turning you down. Managers make their money by commissioning your earnings. If you have no income, they make nothing. Therefore, it is imperative that they use their best efforts to get you a deal.

Publishers

Publishers can be equally as valuable, not only from the standpoint of providing much-needed financial support via advances but also by getting involved in the shopping process. Publishers make their money in a number of ways related to the exploitation of your songs (more on that to be discussed later). Within the realm of record sales, a publisher would recoup his advances to you by the *mechanical income* derived from sales of your record. Therefore, it is most certainly in the publisher's best interest that you secure a record deal; that way, he can recoup his investment in you. Publishers are considered among the most trusted ears in the industry, and many publishers either came from or go to a label in some part of their career. Many times, you will see publishers at the same showcases as A&R reps, and in some cases they are more aggressive in scouting and signing unknown talent than their label counterparts. An A&R rep may be more apt to give serious consideration to a band that has a publishing deal because he knows that the publisher has faith in the band and may even invest additional promotional dollars to help the label promote the band after it's signed.

Once you are confident that your tape and promo package is an accurate and adequate representation of you or your band, try to get it to as many managers and publishers as you can. Check first to make sure that they are accepting material. Some may not want to take on any additional clients, and many publishers have the same "closed-door" policy the labels have, although it's not as bad.

Club Owners

Your local clubs are a valuable resource in the building process. Building a live following is one of the most surefire ways to secure a record deal. More than anything else, major labels want to see how people react to your band. It's like a litmus test, and if it works on a regional level, it'll work on a national level. Many major labels check in with the larger clubs on a regular basis to find out who are the happening bands in a particular region. Also, some clubs report to performance magazines such as *Pollstar*, which lists box office receipts from both national and regional events. If you happen to open up for a national act, your name may be listed alongside the headliners as part of the bill, giving you national exposure. If you become popular enough to headline and draw sellout crowds, label reps will take notice and will undoubtedly start inquiring about this unsigned band that everyone is flocking to see. Therefore, be sure to send your promo kit, complete with demo, photo, and any recent press clippings, to as many club owners as possible. Offer to play for free, just to get the exposure and opportunity to build your following. Any day you're not playing live is a day that you are not increasing your fan base and not allowing yourself to be seen by someone who may help your career.

Record Store Owners and Independent Releases

Never before has the importance of releasing independent product been greater than it is today. Independent records are kind of like the farm system of major league baseball: They can be stepping-stones to the big leagues. By releasing your own albums either on your own or via a small independent label, you prove to the major labels that you have the ability to appeal to a broad spectrum of people. It's like you're saying to them, "Look, even *without* your help, I am able to sell X number of records in X territories around the world. Just imagine the kind of numbers we could do if we were on your major label, given the advantage of working with a professional marketing and promotional department!" Many bands have gotten their start this way: Ratt, Mötley Crüe, and Pantera all released albums on their own labels, and Metallica's first album was for a small, independent company.

In some cases, bands that have success on small labels (sometimes called *indies*) actually decide to stay on that label, even though they may have offers from the majors. Many of these bands feel that they would much rather be the big fish in the small pond rather than the opposite, and that the indie labels are able to devote much more personal attention and effort to their careers. And, surprisingly, it may be in their best financial interest to stay; royalty rates at smaller labels are normally higher than their major label counterparts. Indie labels normally have their own A&R staff, or, at the very least, one person who makes the creative decisions for the company. Again, if you have what you consider an accurate representation of your band, it's in your best interest to try to get it to as many of the indies as possible.

If you have your sights set on a major label deal *only*, then at least get your product out to the local record stores. Ask them if they will sell your release on consignment if they won't buy product outright from you. That way, it's not a financial risk to them. Many stores report to various trade magazines, which are read by the A&R community, and if you sell enough copies, you may be picked up by *Soundscan*, the industry's electronic sales monitoring system. Every major label subscribes to *Soundscan*, and these reports are like an A&R rep's bible, telling him exactly how many pieces of a particular product were sold at any given store at any given time. Reps can tell if there is a certain region that the sales are coming from, or a specific time frame, like after a band's performance in the area. Many of these stores are also contacted by A&R reps directly on a regular basis (to see what local product seems to be attracting attention), so it's real important to have this base covered. Several prominent A&R reps got their start as record store clerks—maybe that's why they trust the opinions of store employees and owners so much! Record stores also tend to be gathering points for hard-core music fans that always want to pick up on the new bands that are out there. One fan tells another, who tells another, who tells another, and so forth. Giving a couple of copies to the clerks who work there wouldn't be a bad idea either, seeing as they may have some influence on the music that is displayed or heard in the store.

Magazines and Fanzines

The print media has traditionally been one of the most important allies in finding and breaking a band. Long before there was MTV or the Internet, there were the stalwart rock magazines like *Rolling Stone, Circus, Hit Parader,* and *Creem.* Some of these magazines started off as regional publications and grew with time. The magazines were the only way you could find out what your favorite band was doing, or see live action photos from the current tour. Today, with the proliferation of cable music programs, satellite TV, late-night talk shows that feature live bands, and, of course, the World Wide Web, we can get a lot of this information instantly. The role of the magazines, while still hugely important, has shifted somewhat.

Many of the major magazines pride themselves on being "cutting edge." That is, they like to feel like they discovered a new band and were the first to recognize their talent. In many cases, this is absolutely true. Today, many of the major mags devote a special column to new, unsigned talent. Until recently, *Metal Edge* magazine had a column called "Rock on the Rise," which featured dozens of bands that were initially unsigned but later went on to secure deals. Pantera is an example of one of those bands, and this author had a hand in getting *Metal Edge* to profile them very early in their career. *Rip* magazine had a similar column called "Buzz Bin," which spotlighted emerging talent, including my own band.

Regional music magazines are usually the first ones to give local bands any press, since it's usually the local music scene they are featuring in the first place. Almost every major metropolitan city has at least one music or entertainment publication. Send your promo kit to the editor or music correspondent. Keep these contacts on your mailing list and update them with any new activity or other press. Invite them to your shows and parties. Offer them some product for giveaways to their readers. Take out ads in these magazines to announce your gigs, even if the clubs may list you in their own ads. The editors will love you for this. Many A&R reps scour the regional magazines, using them as another tool in their search for unmined gold.

Fanzines are magazines started by fans—hence the name. There are hundreds of such fanzines around the United States, ranging from crude, one-page flyers to full-color, bound, glossy publications. Most are run by true fans solely for the pure love of music. Instead of waiting for the major mags to write about their favorite artists, they write about them on their own. And because these fanzines usually don't have any advertising from the major labels, they are not biased in any way and are free to write about *what* they want, and *when*. The readers of these fanzines are usually passionate about the music as well; in fact, sometimes the readers are the only writers the fanzine has! The great thing about fanzines is that they're "of the fans, by the fans, and for the fans," and if you make a fan early on, you'll make a fan for life. Many of these fans interact with others around the country in an informal web, and in a short period of time, what started out as a mention in a small fanzine can blossom into a full-blown press release! The groundswell of support that can be generated is really amazing—both Keel and Cold Sweat owed a lot to fanzines. Get your material out to as many as possible. It's like money in the bank.

Your local newspaper is often a great way to get that first break in ink. Approach the local entertainment writer and ask if he may be interested in doing a human-interest story on you or the band or at least mention you in a column. Remember: *Any press is better than no press.*

Online Services and Web Sites

The advent of the computer age and the growth of the Internet have brought about the most revolutionary change since the beginning of recorded music. It has literally altered the face of the music business in a scant few years, and promises to forever change the way we listen to, and purchase, music. Hundreds of millions of people regularly use the Internet. As computer prices drop and accessibility becomes easier, this number will only increase. It is entirely possible at this very juncture for an artist to completely bypass the structure of the standard record company and make his or her product available electronically to the masses. On top of that, an artist can now be compensated directly from the buying public at profit margins unheard of at any label. The word "independent" has never had a more important meaning: Artists can now record, distribute, and collect compensation without the involvement of a traditional label at all. Granted, there need to be some technological advances before all the quirks are ironed out, but this is only a matter of time.

With the growth of the Internet has come the proliferation of services that act as a "virtual" label. Sound bites of portions or entire songs can be stored on a Web site, along with the artist's biographical material, photos, press releases, and videos. A user can log onto these sites, sample a band's songs, read their press or bio material, and order the band's CD right from the Web site.

Some of these sites charge the artist a fee of some sort, to offset the cost of putting together their portion of the site and the electronic storage and maintenance of it. The providers will normally advertise their sites, both electronically and through standard print media, to make the general public aware of the Web address. The A&R community is well aware of these sites, and they are becoming an increasingly popular way for reps to discover new talent.

Making your own Web site is becoming easier and easier to do and affords even the most novice of computer users the ability to post their own electronic billboard for the world to see. Most everyone knows a computer wizard, who might be more than anxious to help with Web site design and deployment. A creative Web site, which shows off your artistic ability in several media, can spark the attention of a label. Stories have been circulating on various industry message boards about artists who have garnered label interest from Internet activity alone.

Local or College Radio

Along with the local print media, your local radio stations are another way to get the proverbial "foot in the door" and get the ball rolling. Many local radio stations have programs that feature local, unsigned talent. A great example of this is Los Angeles station KLOS, one of the biggest stations on the West Coast. They have a program on Sunday nights called *Local Licks*, which plays only unsigned bands. This program is one of the longest-running ones of its kind in the country: It's been on the air over fifteen years! Many bands have garnered label attention as a result of exposure from the show, and a few have even been signed. Call your local stations and ask if they have a similar program, or if they'd do an interview with the band as a human-interest story. If your community does not have its own station, find out where the closest college radio station is.

College radio has always been a staunch supporter of both local and independent releases, and it has become increasingly important as a tool for the major labels. College radio, like its print media counterpart, is for the most part a very independent medium run *by* music lovers *for* music lovers. College stations in general are very influential to their listeners, and the demographics of these listeners are exactly the demographics the major labels want to target. This is why the major labels pay increasingly more attention to what they're playing. Many college stations now report to the industry radio tipsheets that are read by A&R types, and the performing rights organizations (ASCAP, BMI, and SESAC) are now paying royalties on songs that are broadcast on certain college stations. Several popular college DJs have gone on to be hired as A&R reps and have worked their way up the company ladder.

Contests

In the past few years there has been a proliferation of industry-sponsored contests that showcase new talent. The basic premise of these contests is to discover, expose, and award new talent that has been deemed worthy by the contests' celebrity or industry judges. Some of these, such as the *Billboard Song Contest,* have been long-running affairs that draw thousands of entrants. Others, such as contests sponsored by Ticketmaster or Tanqueray, are more recent and are still developing a following. The winners are usually awarded a cash prize, equipment, or even a contract with a major label or publisher. And although it's not the most typical way, there have been several instances of bands getting a major label deal from a contest. It does provide an opportunity for you to be heard or seen by industry types, so, at the very least, it should be considered a vehicle to get your material heard by these people. Normally there is a nominal fee to enter—it could be anywhere from $10 to $50. Again, you want to make sure that you put your best material on first. The judges will be listening to hundreds of tapes, so you really have to make a statement; you have to be special. Also, be prepared to actually perform your material, since there is usually a grand finale at which the semifinalists will play live.

Star Search, the long-running TV show starring Ed McMahon, was particularly noteworthy for finding some talented people. Sam Harris was the longest-running winning contestant. His soaring vocals and unique arrangements brought him national acclaim. It also brought him a major label record deal, which has since led him to other ventures, including Broadway shows.

Rosie O'Donnell, Dennis Miller, Sinbad, Britney Spears, and LeAnn Rimes are also alumni of this show. *Star Search,* unfortunately, has been cancelled, but Ed McMahon is back with a similar show called *Next Big Star.* Check out the Web site at *www.nextbigstar.com.*

If you don't have either the access or the desire to enter a national contest, at least get involved on a local level—almost every community has a talent show of some sort. The experience and exposure can only do you good. Take it from me: I won third place in a local show when I was fourteen and put $100 in my pocket in the process!

A Friend of a Friend of a Brother-in-Law's Cousin's Stepsister's Ex-College Roommate

Fate has a strange way of altering the best-laid plans, sometimes for better, sometimes for worse. You may follow every one of the above ideas but still not get to that *one* right person. You may send out 1,001 promo kits, blanket the local, regional, and national music business community in the process, and still not make that *one* connection. In the end, it may be a combination of things or a single, unforeseen event that puts you in touch with the right person. Bottom line: *Get your demo out to anyone and everyone*—you never know who's related to who or who knows who by way of whoever. Life is full of coincidences. Make them work in your favor. Be sure that you are absolutely prepared for that moment when an act of fate presents itself. You may be in the checkout line in the local supermarket or sitting two seats away on an airplane from the president of a record company. You may be at a restaurant or club when in walks a famous rock star who just formed his own label. Or maybe your sister's best friend just happens to be babysitting for the hottest record producer on the planet.

It's just a matter of time before some crazy scenario presents itself. You *have* to be ready. It may literally be the chance of a lifetime, and you can't afford to let it pass you by. If fate opens a door, you want to be damn sure you're there not only to get your foot in, but to bust that door down. Make sure you keep a few promo kits with you at *all* times, either in your car or in your carry-on bag. Have a supply of business cards with you, as well as pen and paper. The more prepared, the better. A battle was never won by an unprepared army—don't stack the odds against yourself. Everyone has a destiny, but you *can* control your fate to some degree.

CHAPTER 3
Signed, Sealed, and Delivered:
Getting That Record Deal

Getting your demo heard and your performance seen by the right people can be an extremely frustrating experience. At times, you may feel like you're trying to row a boat upstream with one oar, or you're taking one step forward and two steps back. The odds are certainly stacked against you, and it might seem like *nobody* wants to give you a break. It's times like these that build character, stamina, and humility. But it's also a time that helps build the toughness that a lot of artists need to maintain a career in the music industry. This outer shell can act as a defensive barrier in dealing with the industry, because, as I mentioned before, labels oftentimes view artists as disposable product. You're a valuable commodity to them if you're making money, but if not, you're a financial liability. Think of these hard times as "musical boot camp"—if you survive these hardships, you'll come out a better, stronger, tougher person. And while I certainly don't think that anyone should *have* to suffer through hard times, it's a foregone conclusion that most artistic people do, and this process helps shape their creative soul, for better or for worse.

As I said earlier, when Keel started, we rehearsed seven days a week in a tiny roach-infested warehouse in the middle of gang territory. Several band members had their cars stolen and their lives threatened. The five of us became tough as nails in the process, and it helped instill in us a sense of "us against the world," not only against our immediate surroundings but also against the industry. I am fully convinced that this attitude helped insulate us against a lot of the unpleasant business practices we would have to deal with later on.

Let's assume you have done everything in your power to get your music into the hands of someone who can help advance your career. You have further helped your cause by making yourself as visible as possible by playing live constantly, saturating the local press and airwaves, manufacturing and marketing your own product, and making your presence known on the Internet. You've never worked so hard or so passionately in your whole life. You're devoting every fiber of your being and spending any extra dollar you have on the advancement of your career. You're blocking out any negative thoughts and focusing positive, creative energy on the prospect of achieving your lofty goal. Everyone and his mother is behind you 1,000 percent, telling their friends and strangers about you, spreading the good word like wildfire. You know in your heart that you are ready, and you are just praying for an opportunity to show the world what *you* already know—that you're a star.

One day later, you come home to a message on your answering machine. It's from the head of A&R at a major company. Apparently, his dog groomer's sister's boyfriend's kid brother gave him your tape as he was picking up his pooch. He threw it in the car stereo on the ride home and almost caused a fourteen-car collision when he was knocked out by the power of your musical onslaught. He called you from his car phone because he couldn't take the chance of not being the first one to inquire about the band. He thinks the tape is the most incredible piece of musical work since *Sgt. Pepper* and if you can pull it off live, you'll be signing your name on the dotted line in no time! Well, of course you can play live—you've done 350 shows in the past 365 days, and the band is tighter than Scrooge at Christmastime. One day later, you arrange a private showcase for him, proceed to blow his socks off, and boom—the next morning he faxes a deal memo to your attorney.

Hello! Time to wake up now, class. Daydreaming 101 is over. It's back to the real world. While it is conceivable that a scenario such as the one detailed above can actually happen (and perhaps a similar one has), in reality the signing process is much more protracted and grueling. Normally, an A&R rep will express a subtle interest in the band, ask to hear more material, see the band perform in front of a live audience, and at the same time check out the band's numbers at retail: Do they have independent product out? Where are they selling—regionally or nationally? What kind of numbers? Are they getting airplay? Or, he may forward your tape to a producer he's worked with before to get an opinion. If the producer confers with him, hey, maybe it's worth a shot to do a *demo deal* first.

DEMO DEALS

A demo deal is what the name implies. A label will put the band into the studio at the company's cost to hear some new material that you may have. If the label likes the outcome, it will have the option to sign you, normally within a certain period of time—say, thirty to sixty days from completion of the demo. If they elect to pass on you, you may then have the option of approaching or signing with other labels. It's like a "try before you buy" policy. Some artists are dead set against demo deals. Some view demo deals as a means of stalling: Their line of thinking is that the label should like what it hears *now* and make the commitment to them immediately—no pussy-footing around.

If you don't have a lot of other labels to choose from, then a demo deal may be your only option, and one you should accept willingly. Hey, at the very least you'll get some studio time on their dime. *Make sure that you maintain ownership of the recordings (and the songs) if they decide to pass on you.* That way you can use the recordings for other submissions or uses, such as film and TV work.

BIDDING WARS

If, by chance, you *do* have interest from more than one label, you are in an enviable situation. Having more than one suitor puts you in a better negotiating position. Just like at an auction, if an item generates a lot of interest, more people are apt to be bidding, driving the price up. In the record industry, a *bidding war* is what occurs when several labels go after the same band, thereby pitting themselves against each other, like wolves fighting over the same carcass. When this phenomenon occurs, the artist is in a great position to demand better terms and deal points. The more a label wants you, the more concessions they will make to sign you. You may be able to secure a better advance, a higher royalty rate, a longer commitment in the form of guaranteed releases, or perhaps an increase in video monies or tour support. As long as you're able to take advantage of this situation, you should milk it for all it's worth because the money you get now may be the only money you ever get from the label.

An observation about bidding wars in general: Bidding wars tend to put a lot of unwanted hype and pressure on bands. The press almost inevitably gets wind of this escalating bidding and touts the band as the "next big thing." All of a sudden, there are such built-up expectations that the band must live up to, but never asked for. Most of the bands that were the subjects of big-name bidding wars over the past ten years never lived up to these expectations and in many cases disbanded after an album or two. One band, Guns n' Roses, managed to buck the trend and even surpass all the hoopla that surrounded them, but that was a rarity.

Therefore, whether or not to inform the A&R community about interest from one label is a debatable point. As I mentioned earlier: Interest breeds interest. If an A&R person finds out that someone is sniffing about a band, it automatically piques his curiosity: "*Why* is someone else interested in this band, and *why* didn't I know about it first?" So, on the one hand, you want everyone to know that *someone* is interested in you, perhaps setting the bidding war in motion. But on the other hand, you don't want to come off as too anxious or plotting—that may piss off the people who are genuinely interested in signing you. My advice would be to discreetly plant some gossip in the trades or on the Internet about the impending signing of your band—just a little anonymous teaser that links your name and the prospective label. This should fan the flames just enough without making too many waves—a little catalyst to get things brewing, if you will. A&R reps *love* to see their name in print. It's almost an affirmation of purpose to them. By the way, there are enough "spies" in the industry to tip one record company off to the other anyway, so secrets are not well kept!

ENTERING NEGOTIATIONS AND THE COURTING PROCESS

When people court you, they'll say almost anything to get you. Whether it's love or business, sometimes things are said in the pursuit of passion that may not hold true after the passion dies. You will hear things like, "The label is committed to making you a priority," "Everyone from the president on down *loves* the band," "We have devised the biggest marketing plan *ever* for the album," "Save a spot on your wall for the platinum album," "Start shopping for the house on the beach," or even, "You're a shoo-in for a Grammy." I've heard all these and more in my day. Like a lover making a fervent vow, words can roll off the tongue without the intention of ever keeping the promise. Therefore, it is important that you take things with a grain of salt when prospective suitors make promises. This is the honeymoon period when everything is just beautiful, when everybody is on their best behavior and everyone is all smiles, but after the honeymoon is over, band and label have to get down to honoring the marriage, and we all know that marriage takes a lot of hard work.

When entering into actual negotiations, you want to make sure you get all these promises in writing. You want a *concrete* dollar number for videos, tour support, promotional items, independent radio marketing, and outside press. With videos running anywhere from $50,000 on up, touring costs beginning at $10,000 per week, independent press in the neighborhood of $5,000 per month (radio pluggers almost twice that), and promotional costs even greater, all of a sudden, you are becoming a very expensive date! Most of these costs are *recoupable,* meaning that in the end, *you* are actually paying for all this, unless you can negotiate for a portion of these costs to be nonrecoupable. You want to negotiate for as many *guaranteed* releases as possible. Just because you sign a seven-album deal doesn't mean the label is going to *release* all seven albums—they just have the option to do so. If you become a successful artist who sells a great deal of product, it is likely the label will want to keep you under contract and release as many albums as it can. If you're a flop, the label may cut you loose after one album. I know of a few bands that were signed to a major label and recorded their debut album. Then, the label shelved the album, refused to release it, and dropped the band.

SINKING THE SHIP BEFORE IT LEAVES THE SHORE

Why on earth would a label go to such expense to court a band, spend thousands upon thousands to record the album, prepare artwork, develop a marketing strategy (sometimes up to the point of prepurchasing ads), and then pull the plug on the whole thing? There are a few typical reasons for this:

> The label felt that the final version of the record was too far removed from what it thought it was going to be and lost interest in the project. This is a lame excuse, because normally the label *knows* the artist it is signing, has heard the artist on demos, and has had at least a little input in the recording process. However, this excuse has been used on more than one occasion.

> Something fundamentally wrong happened, which changed the relationship between artist and label. Perhaps a drug problem surfaced, or mental problems or extreme personal or family problems arose, which might prevent the artist from following through on promoting or touring behind the album. The label would therefore feel that it would be cutting its losses by not releasing the album.

The person who signed the band was fired or left the label. In the beginning, your A&R rep is your most important ally at the label. Many times, he is the one who brought the band into the label in the first place and is responsible for firing up the other departments to get excited about the band. A lot of times, the A&R rep is the *only* person who believes in the band at first, and he has to win over other people's confidence. He is like your tooth fairy, big brother, godfather, and right-hand man all rolled into one. If he leaves or is fired, odds are the band will have no one else to carry the torch. This is a very unfortunate circumstance, but it happens more often than it should. If you are able to, try to negotiate a *key man clause*, which stipulates that you would be able to be released from your contract and have the ability to follow your A&R rep (or label president) over to where he winds up. It may be difficult for a new band to negotiate this, as this clause is normally reserved for huge recording artists who have already had long careers. These artists may have a pre-existing relationship with the president or A&R rep, and that's the only reason they're at the label to begin with. It doesn't hurt to ask for it, though; it can help save a career.

The label itself goes under or is taken over by another label—another sad circumstance that one hopes never happens, but that unfortunately does. A little preventive research into the fiscal health of a prospective label or some monitoring of the industry rumor mills may turn out to be a career saver. You wouldn't want to buy a house that was about to collapse or a car that was about to die, so why *knowingly* get involved with a label that may face financial instability? We all want a record deal, but it has to be under the right circumstances.

DON'T GET YOURSELF TRAPPED!
••

A pearl of wisdom for you: *Having no deal is better than having a bad deal.* Don't rush into a record contract. Getting *out* of a record contract can be one of the most difficult, costly, time-consuming, legally complicated things you could ever do. It can literally ruin your career. The labels have an army of attorneys who work for them, both in-house and independently on retainer. They are much better prepared to wait out a legal battle; time is on their side, not yours. If you're out of the public spotlight, you are forgotten. Don't be like an animal caught in a leg trap, enduring a life of pain and agony. That dotted line can wait a little bit until you're confident that you've negotiated the best possible terms for yourself. After all, it's *your* career.
••

The record contract is like the "brass ring" or the "golden chalice" that so many chase but so few catch. It is thought of as the ultimate trophy of one's musical quest and a passport to wealth, fame, and glory. Many naïve artists think that just because they sign a major label deal, their problems are over, but in actuality, their problems are just beginning. With a major label deal, you are no longer a big fish in the little pond, but rather a tiny fish in a huge ocean. What most don't realize, however, is that your standard record industry contract, all sixty-plus pages in its gleaming white glory, is actually one of the most lopsided business agreements on Planet Earth. Lurking within those pages are enough clauses, conditions, limitations, and provisions to ensure that all but the most successful recording artists never see a dime past their initial advances. These terms are so weighted in the record company's favor from so many different angles that recording artists barely stand a chance of ever breaking even. Among legal professionals a standard record contract is widely perceived as being one step up from indentured servitude.

CHOOSING YOUR ATTORNEY

In light of the complexities of your standard record company contract, it is imperative that you have an attorney whom you trust to negotiate on your behalf. This attorney should be one who has an emphasis in entertainment law, as this is a specialized part of law. Even though you may have an uncle who handles personal injury or bankruptcies and has offered to look over your contract, politely decline and hire a music attorney. You wouldn't want a dentist performing open-heart surgery. Sure, a dentist may know the fundamentals of the human body, and perhaps even a little about the cardiovascular system, but he doesn't specialize in that exact field. Music law is an animal unto itself, and it requires someone who is familiar with its stripes. It may cost you more now, but it will save you in the long run. You should choose someone who has had experience with the label in question, or perhaps one who has been known to negotiate better deals for his clients. Talk to other bands and see who they're working with. If you get to the point of being the big fish in the little pond, it's quite possible that some attorneys may contact *you*. Attorneys sniff out the hot bands, too; they know that these bands are eventually going to need legal services, and it's best to get to them at an early stage.

If you happen to get involved with an attorney who actually shopped your tape on your behalf and through his efforts secured you a deal, you should know that there might be the possibility of a conflict of interest. Although it may not be apparent, the attorney in question may not always have your best interests in mind in negotiating a deal in which he stands to make a cut of the advance. He may sacrifice a bigger back end for the front end, knowing that he will commission up-front monies. In other words, he may get you a bigger advance now (one that he commissions) at the expense of smaller tour support or video budgets. Also, he may not be as aggressive in negotiating certain points because there are other bands he wants to present to the label, and he doesn't want to push too hard for fear of becoming a nuisance. I don't want to imply that this type of behavior is the norm, but it has undoubtedly happened and is a cause for precaution.

A funny anecdote: A good friend of mine was in a band signed to WTG/Sony Records. Being Scottish, he had the requisite Scottish brogue and was a little difficult to understand when he spoke fast or after he had had a few drinks. One day, we got to talking about record deals, and he mentioned to me that he had just hooked up with a great "liar." This "falsifier" had helped his band get a great record deal and

Cold Sweat signing our record contract with MCA Records.
Courtesy Marc Ferrari.

a lucrative publishing deal as well. On top of that, this fibber, whom I was being led to believe was prone to never telling the whole truth, had also hooked the band up with a nifty merchandising advance. Well, I had always been raised to be honest and be on the up-and-up, but I was getting intrigued as to how someone could lie his way into all these lucrative deals without any repercussions. So I asked my friend just who this guy was. "He's a new liar with the firm of ———. Here's his number." This was years before the movie *Liar Liar* was released, by the way.

CHAPTER 4

Building the Team: Attorneys, Managers, Agents, Accountants . . . Who Needs 'Em, Anyhow?

Unfortunately, it's not enough to be talented or creative; you have to have a business sense as well. And you should never lose sight of the fact that the record industry *is* a huge business of which you are but a microcosm. You are a business onto yourself, and your business has to compete against others, all the while functioning within the framework of the big picture. When you're playing on a major label level, it sometimes gets to the point where the business aspects of your work seem to override the musical aspects. Business responsibilities often cut into and interfere with creative responsibilities. It's an unfortunate circumstance, but one every musician has to accept. The key is to find the balance between commerce and art and to surround yourself with a contingent of competent, trustworthy people. They will be with you side by side in battle.

Attorneys, managers, producers, business managers, tour managers, agents, publicists, A&R reps—these are all components of "the team" that surrounds your business entity. Like a president choosing his cabinet members, these are the key people you trust to advise you, guide you, and sometimes make decisions on your behalf. They each have a specific yet separate function, and, with the exception of the A&R rep, *they are all hired directly by you!*

YOUR ATTORNEY

Your attorney is the cornerstone of your team. Strictly as a provider of legal services, he is responsible for reviewing all contracts, agreements, licenses, and other business proposals. He will negotiate on your behalf the best possible terms and conditions, act as a mediator between parties, and prepare legal documents for you to sign. In some cases your attorney can act as a soliciting agent on your behalf, and he may approach prospective labels, publishers, or merchandising companies to do deals. He offers advice on career moves, can act as your spokesperson, and in some cases takes on the role of a manager. In fact, many bands that don't have a manager or are between managers will have their attorney manage the group. Most attorneys charge an hourly rate for their services, billing anywhere from $50 to $500 per hour, and they are usually hired on a noncontractual basis. This means that you can fire them if you're dissatisfied and, as long as you pay off your bill, you are able to hire someone else without legal ramifications.

YOUR MANAGER

A manager is a funny breed, a hybrid of sorts—part businessperson, part personal confidant, part psychiatrist, part tyrant, part banker, part magician, and, sometimes, part lunatic. The fundamental role of a manager is to handle the day-to-day affairs of overseeing your career and to offer advice on career advancement. That in itself can entail a wide range of obligations and responsibilities, since there are so many different pieces that make up the music business puzzle. It is extremely important to know that *anybody* in the world can call himself a manager. There are no tests to pass, no associations to belong to, no licenses to earn, and no regulatory agencies that govern the activities of managers. Doctors, lawyers, accountants, psychiatrists, social workers, and other service-related professionals all must go through years of intensive schooling, testing, and interning just to start practicing. Furthermore, many of these professionals must adhere to strict guidelines and codes of ethics to be members in good standing, and they can be censured, punished, and penalized if found to be unscrupulous. Managers have a free rein to do almost anything related to your career, and it is truly amazing that there is no agency that regulates the power that is vested in them.

Tim Collins managed the rock band Aerosmith for over twelve years. When he took the band on in 1984, they were nearly bankrupt, on the brink of self-destruction, and without a record deal. He helped guide the band to perhaps the greatest comeback in rock history, restoring the band to multiplatinum international acclaim. The band recently signed one of the most lucrative recording contracts ever and has reestablished itself as a powerhouse in the recording industry. I first met Tim in 1982, when I was living in the Boston area and playing in cover bands. He became a great friend and mentor to me, and later, after I had been signed with Keel, a trusted adviser. Tim once said something to me that I have never forgotten: A bad manager could do more harm than a bad doctor, and could never be punished for it. Given the lack of supervision, intervention, or regulation for managers, these words carry an added weight: *Be extremely cautious in choosing a manager, because, unlike an attorney, you will be bound by a contract.*

Standard management contracts usually start with an initial period of two years, with one-year options that can extend the contract to seven years. Make sure that these options are mutually agreed upon; otherwise, it will be the manager's decision alone to keep you on. If he is doing a good job, you'll want to keep him on, but if not, you'll want to have the option to terminate the contract. Many artists have a *performance clause* built into their management contract that stipulates that the manager must earn the client a certain amount of gross income per year in order to exercise an option period. If the manager does not meet this performance mark, the artist would then be able to terminate the agreement at the end of that current period. This is an effective safety net and certainly should encourage the manager to meet the mark and put more dollars in your pocket.

Managers usually work on a commission basis. The usual range is 15 percent to 25 percent of your gross income, with 20 percent being the norm. Of course, this is negotiable, as well as *which* monies the manager will commission. Typically, managers will commission record advances (but not record *budgets*), publishing and merchandising advances, endorsement advances, and touring income. Video budgets, tour support, and promotional monies are not normally commissionable and should be stated as such in your contract.

Managers will attempt to receive commissions in perpetuity for deals that were in place at the time they were managing you. Consider a scenario in which your current manager is instrumental in getting you a record deal. He deserves to be compensated, and rightly so. He takes 20 percent of your advance right off the bat. You fire him after two years. The album is still selling well and earning you income, but technically he doesn't manage you any more. The manager feels that because he was instrumental in getting the deal in the first place, he should continue to be compensated. After all, *you're* still earning money off it, as well as off the subsequent publishing deal. However, *you* feel otherwise. Sure, perhaps it was his initial efforts that got you the deal, but the public is buying *your* album, not his—you're the star that everyone wants. Hopefully, here's where your attorney made his money by negotiating favorable terms in your management agreement. Many managers will insist on this perpetuity clause, but, like everything else, it is negotiable, so try to have this time period limited to a few years after termination of the agreement.

Meanwhile, below are some of the major functions a manager should perform:

Helping to Secure Record, Publishing, and Merchandise Deals

If you sign on with a manager before you have a record deal, your manager may be very instrumental in helping you secure a deal. He or she may help set up showcases or private auditions with various labels or perhaps get you onto a high-profile show at a local venue opening up for a national act. Your manager may have a close relationship with a label president or A&R rep and may be able to call in some heavy favors to get you signed. Or, perhaps your manager already handles a high-profile national act and can use this as leverage to get you a contract. This same leverage may also apply to publishing or merchandising deals. Your manager should have a lot of contacts in the music business and have the ability to use these contacts to forward your career.

Finding Work

A manager can be very helpful in finding ancillary employment in other music-related fields, such as sideline work with other recording projects, film and TV composing, acting, or live performances. It should be noted that in some states, such as California, it is illegal for your manager to be your booking agent as well. The manager can *call* a booking agent on your behalf, but he cannot actually book you.

Serving as an Artist Liaison

Another important function your manager serves is acting as your liaison or spokesperson. Your manager acts as a buffer between you and the record company and others. If something is not going properly with the making, marketing, or promotion of your album, it is the manager's responsibility to make the effort to see that it gets rectified. A good manager stays in constant contact with the label throughout the marketing campaign, making sure the label is doing its job in getting your record out to retail and radio. Getting involved with the campaign strategy, the implementation, and its subsequent follow-through is an important ingredient in a successful record. Sometimes a manager will have to get aggressive with a particular staff member to make sure that everything is going smoothly. It would be highly improper for an artist to do this; therefore, your manager acts as the "bad guy" or "fall guy" in this regard.

Your manager can also act as your spokesperson in times of trouble or crisis, handling tasks like fielding calls from the press and shielding you from unwanted nuisances. Issuing press statements and fending off those inquisitive tabloid journalists come with the territory. Just remember your poor manager back at the office the next time you get involved in an international scandal! This brings up another topic: the manager as a mediator. As mentioned earlier, the term *manager* is a catch-all phrase, which doesn't come with a defined job description. Sometimes a manager has to get involved with an artist on a personal level. He may not be *asked* to get involved (nor may he *want* to get involved), but sometimes he just *has* to. If there is a serious intraband squabble or fight, the manager may act as a go-between, or "referee," if you will. He may be a more neutral party, better able to see the big picture than individual band members, who may bring personal agendas to an issue. Don't forget that artists tend to be emotional, temperamental, and prone to overreaction by nature. Having someone with a clear vision and an unbiased stance on an issue can help alleviate a problem that could very easily get out of hand.

Our manager in Keel, Tim Heyne, was very effective in being the water that put out the flame on many occasions. Cooler heads always prevail, and in the heat of the argument, the band manager can be the firefighter who saves the burning building. Other times, a manager is simply a friend: someone you go to when you need to vent frustrations or express anxieties, someone to share a moment of laughter with, someone to turn to for advice, someone to hit up for a personal loan, someone to watch your back. I know several managers who have intervened with clients when they had substance abuse problems, who have been largely responsible for literally saving their clients' lives. It's times like these that the business relationship takes a backseat to the human relationship. Commissions don't mean a thing if an artist can't perform his functions.

However, managers aren't supposed to be full-time babysitters. They should not be asked to constantly mediate arguments or disagreements, with band members acting like spoiled children crying to their mommies. Their main function, rather, is to advance your career by doing what they're supposed to be doing. If a manager is constantly pulled away from important business by trivial matters, it only hurts the band. Hopefully you can work out your differences internally.

YOUR BUSINESS MANAGER

Strictly speaking, the role of a business manager is to control the day-to-day functions of your business entity. The business manager's responsibilities include setting up the band business (e.g., a partnership, a limited partnership, or a corporation), establishing bank accounts for the band, receiving royalty payments and other income, and dispersing funds. The business manager really earns his keep when an artist is on the road. When an artist is touring, there is a great deal of financial activity that happens on a daily basis. Wire transfers may come in as payment from a concert, and various salaries must be paid out. Emergency money may be needed at a moment's notice, and other vendors such as those establishing lighting, sound equipment, or tour bus rentals may need to get paid. Insurance for the tour must be acquired, and in the event of international touring, complex tax issues must be dealt with. Most business managers are either CPAs (Certified Public Accountants), CFPs (Certified Financial Planners), or a combination of both. Both CPAs and CFPs must be licensed and certified to practice, and they must carry bond insurance. Bands and solo artists are mini-businesses unto themselves, and in the case of major artists, they can become multimillion-dollar-a-year operations, employing dozens of people. Handling payroll, taxes, health insurance, and other financial matters is a task that only a financial specialist should be involved with.

Business managers are paid either an hourly rate or a percentage of the gross earnings of the business. This arrangement can work either to the artist's advantage or disadvantage, depending on the size of the business and what the hourly rate is. A smaller band with little income may opt to pay the percentage (normally 5 percent), and may save over the hourly rate.

However, a multiplatinum band would wind up paying a lot more on a percentage arrangement and therefore would actually benefit from an hourly rate. Normally, business managers prefer the percentage arrangement. In the beginning, when a band first starts out, there is not a lot of work the business manager needs to do. If the band does little or no touring, then there won't be a lot of billing hours to the client. In the eyes of the business manager, the percentage arrangement allows his company's billings to be commensurate with the earnings of the band. If the band succeeds, so does the management company. Besides, a business manager may save his clients money by negotiating better rates with certain vendors or by reducing the client's tax liability. Bands themselves usually take a different view: Why should they give a percentage of their overall earnings to someone who is strictly providing a service and not necessarily helping them *make* that money? Well, as with everything else in life, there are compromises. An arrangement that is percentage-based up to a cap would be a possible solution.

YOUR PUBLICIST

You've heard the expression "darlings of the press." Hype can be a musical artist's best friend. Unfortunately for those who rely strictly on sheer musical talent to sell records, hype can sell more albums than talent. Just like a successful political campaign manipulates the press to its advantage, publicity is a crucial element in breaking a band. As an image is such an important factor in the music business, it is essential that bands obtain the maximum exposure possible from the media, whether it is from print, radio, television, or the Internet. All major labels have their own publicity departments. Their function is to coordinate publicity campaigns, arrange interviews, and (subject to the artist's schedule and approval), book certain public appearances. While most of the labels do a good job of promoting their artists *in-house* (from within the label), many artists feel they do not want to compete with other artists on the roster and therefore decide to hire an independent publicist to work in conjunction with, or independent of, the label. A publicist can come up with a "spin" or an angle that the media can use to build up an image, aura, or persona for the artist, hopefully increasing the hype factor.

Publicists also use their other clients to *cross-promote*. In other words, if a publicist represents another band that has an event going on, she will encourage other clients to attend the event, get their picture taken with the celebs who may be there, then circulate these photos to the various magazines, news shows, and so on. When Keel was first starting out, we were mostly unknown outside the Los Angeles area. Our publicist was very aggressive in getting our press releases and photos to every possible magazine and periodical and made sure that we were invited to any industry event that might garner media attention. My first photo in a national publication was a shot with Bryan Adams taken at a charity event. This photo was published even *before* our major label debut was released. This started the whole advance hype process, which continued throughout the marketing campaign for our first release. We endeavored to cooperate with our publicist's efforts and made the rounds of parties, premieres, and social events of the day. Even if we weren't famous at the time, by being seen with those who *were*, we became famous by association.

Resulting mostly from our publicist's relationship with the press, we were able to get exposure in many magazines that typically featured bands of bigger stature than we had at the time. Once these magazines hit the stands, readers inquired about these new faces. Other magazines then wanted to feature us as well, and thus began a snowball effect that worked in our favor. One year later, we were voted "Best New Band" in three of the four top rock magazines of the time: *Circus, Metal Edge,* and *Rock Scene.* I am fully convinced that if we hadn't invested in our publicist, we would not have achieved the notoriety that we did in such a short time.

Hype is essential, but does not always come cheap. The typical independent publicist charges a monthly fee, anywhere between $500 to $5,000 per month, depending on the size of the client, the workload involved, and bills for expenses such as postage, telephone calls, and office supplies. Sometimes, a label will pick up a portion of or all of these fees as part of the band's promotional budget, but if they don't, the artist must pay them. Strictly viewed as an investment in one's career, however, independent publicity usually pays back "dollars on the dime."

When choosing a publicist, you'll want to take into consideration several factors. Does the publicist have a proven track record? Does she understand your type of music? Does she have

Keel 1985. A&M Records publicity photo.
Photo credit: Aaron Rapoport. Courtesy A&M Records.

DWAIN MILLER   MARC FERRARI   RON KEEL   BRYAN JAY   KENNY CHAISSON

Keel 1986. MCA Records publicity photo.
Photo credit: Neil Zlozower. Courtesy MCA Records.

MARC FERRARI   BRYAN JAY   RON KEEL   KENNY CHAISSON   DWAIN MILLER

Keel 1987. MCA Records publicity photo.
Photo credit: Michael Ruppert. Courtesy MCA Records.

a roster of well-known clients? Is she properly staffed to serve your needs? Does she have clients in other fields such as film and TV whom she can introduce you to? Does she have a concept or game plan to market you?

And remember: You can never be too famous! Publicity can be a band's best friend. Keel had the advantage of both independent and in-house publicity departments working for us.

YOUR BOOKING AGENT

Booking agents are a behind-the-scenes cog in the wheel. While not normally in the spotlight like a manager, they are an integral part of the machinery. Their chief responsibility is to book the band tour dates. There are five or six major agencies in the United States, but several smaller ones have proved to be very effective. There are only a limited number of national tours going on at any given moment, and when a band is starting out, it is a major coup to secure an opening slot on a big tour. If an agency represents some of the larger acts that are headlining, it can use its influence to try to get you on that tour. As agencies work on a commission basis, (normally 10 percent of gross tour receipts), it is to their benefit to use this influence.

Many of the larger agencies, such as CAA, ICM, and William Morris, have divisions that represent actors, screenwriters, and authors as well. This can work to your benefit, as your agent may be able to keep you in mind for acting jobs or book deals, should the situation warrant it. Keel was represented by ICM, which also represented many actors. We were able to use this synergy and got to be guest stars on a popular TV show at the time called *Throb*. *Throb* was a sitcom based around a record company, and we made a guest appearance as a visiting band. It was our first time on a network TV show, and while it didn't earn us an Emmy, it helped increase our visibility and it was a great experience.

YOUR PRODUCER

One of the most important assets an artist can have is an identifiable *sound*. This sound can become a trademark that the public identifies with the artist, that sets the artist apart as its own unique entity. Just as painters aspire to have their own "look," musical artists strive to achieve their own individual sonic fingerprint. Granted, a part of this sound is due to an artist's unique approach to songwriting and playing. However, the technical aspect of capturing these performances on tape and physically making the product is a science unto itself. It even has a name: *recording science* (or audio engineering). From a strictly technical standpoint, the recording process is extremely involved and demanding. Not only does it require in-depth knowledge of acoustics, electronics, and sound waves, but it also demands that one keep up with ever-changing signal-processing equipment and new technologies. Record making in itself is a craft, and there are those who devote an entire lifetime to the development and perfection of this craft. Music, however, is much more than just the physical sound waves—it is the emotion and passion contained in the song and in the *performance* of the song.

There are three distinct roles a producer plays. First, he acts as the coordinator of the entire recording process. This includes working with the band before it enters the studio, which is known as *preproduction*. In preproduction, the band rehearses the material, makes adjustments to the arrangement and structure of the songs, and chooses which songs are to be recorded. Since many producers come from a musical background, this is a valuable element that the producer brings to the project. Producers have even been known to write songs with artists. A prime example would be Mutt Lange, who wrote many songs with Def Leppard, whom he also produced. Concerning the issue of song selection, the producer may have some input from the label's A&R rep, but in the case of famous producers, this decision may be left up to them. Also, the producer is sometimes responsible for the budgeting of the album and may also assist in the hiring of additional musicians and the renting of certain equipment or of the studio itself.

The second role the producer plays is that of overseeing the *physical* recording process. This includes setting up the equipment and microphones, getting the proper sounds from the equipment, ensuring that the correct levels of audio go to tape, adding the right sound effects, and blending all the tracks together in proper balance for the final mix. He may have an assistant called an *engineer* who may help with this physical process. Often, engineers are the ones who are actually running the cables all over the studio, lugging around the equipment, servicing the tape machines, and performing various maintenance functions. An engineer may have an assistant himself, known as the *second engineer,* or just the *second.* Oftentimes, engineers and seconds are up-and-coming producers in training, like an apprenticeship. They can work their way up the ladder and eventually become full-fledged producers themselves.

Producers must know the language of a musician, as they are frequently asked to interpret what a musician hears in his head, but sometimes semantics of words makes it extremely difficult to translate an idea in one's brain onto a piece of recording tape. A popular story surrounds Eddie Kramer, the renowned producer who worked with Jimi Hendrix. It seems that Hendrix asked Kramer to find a sound that made his guitar sound like it was under water. After Kramer laboriously found the appropriate sound, Hendrix said, "Now make it *blue* water"!

The third role concerns the *emotional* aspect of the recording process. Capturing the right performance is a crucial part of the recording process. In this respect, the producer must develop an intimate relationship with the artist and become a trusted confidant. A lot of times the artist is too close to the process to make an unbiased decision. He may *think* he sang something in tune or played an awesome guitar part, but in reality it was subpar compared to what he *could* achieve. It's like looking in the mirror—all you see is yourself and not what's beyond the mirror or directly behind you. So, having an outside set of ears is extremely important. A good producer knows how to inspire an artist to reach deep into his soul and find the resolve to pull out a passionate performance. Sometimes passages must be repeated dozens of times before the *right* performance occurs. The artist may need that special inspiration to continue redoing something over and over, and here's where the emotional aspect of the producer's job comes into play. A good producer knows when an artist has exhausted his creative energy or becomes too tired or uninspired to continue recording. Like a director of a movie, the producer may decide that this is the time to "call it a day" and pick up again when people are fresh.

Owing to the spiritual bond that may ensue, producers very often become a "phantom" or "additional" member of a band. The perfect example would be George Martin, who became the "fifth Beatle." He was chiefly responsible for capturing the Beatles' unique talents and interpreting their musical ideas. Without his involvement, the Beatles would not have been able to achieve all the glorious groundbreaking studio work they were known for. Martin was not only a technical wizard, but also a trusted adviser and father figure to the group. It's no wonder they worked with him even throughout their solo careers and on the recent *Anthology* series. Another example of a unique artist-producer bond would be Bill Ham and Z.Z. Top. They go back over thirty years together! He has been their only producer throughout their entire career.

Although most artist-producer relationships are productive and amicable, there have been exceptions. Friction can develop when the artist's vision of the project doesn't sync with that of the producer. Sometimes, the producer may be acting under orders from the label to make a record sound a certain way. Perhaps the producer is known for a certain style or sound, and the label feels that this is exactly what the artist needs.

However, what the label feels the artist *needs* and what the artist himself *wants* can be two entirely different things. Sometimes these differences can boil over into confrontations. I've seen it escalate to near fisticuffs proportions. Producers, much like artists, are passionate about their work, and the album is a representation of their work as well.

What happens if the producer and artist are so far apart in vision or ideology that they can't even stand to be in the same room with each other? Whose position is the correct one in these circumstances? Let me answer that question with another question: Just *whose* album is it, anyway? If there's one thing I learned from this situation it's this: Ultimately, it's the artist who must live with the record. It's the *artist's* name on the album, and fans buy the CDs for the artist, not for the producer. Albums are forever, and if an artist isn't happy with it, he has to bear that for eternity, wearing that album like a tattoo of an ex-girlfriend's name. After this album project is over, the producer will more than likely go on to other projects. However, the artist must then go out and support this album for what may be years. He is "married" to the final product much more so than the producer, or even the label. And another thing: It's the artist who ultimately pays for the recording of his *own* album. Don't forget: The recording budget is recoupable from any future royalties. It really is the *artist's* album in so many ways. Now I'm not saying that artists are always right in every situation, but when it comes to major issues like musical direction, the artist's feelings should be given heavier consideration.

It must also be noted that in most cases, the producer will side with the artist. Most producers are "artist-friendly" and are sympathetic to the artist's musical wants and desires. Bear in mind that producers have a vested interest in the success of the record, and they want the artist to be happy with the end result. Happy artists are more prone to go out and support the album for longer lengths of time, increasing album sales, which benefit the producers as well.

Producers receive a fee for their services in the form of a guaranteed payment, a back-end royalty, or a combination of both. A well-known producer on a major label project can command a salary in the range of $25,000 to $150,000 and receive three to seven *points* as a royalty. On a CD that retails for $14.99, this can equal out to 45 cents to over $1 for each record sold. Producers are generally paid from *record one,* which means they get paid from the first record sold, regardless of whether the band has recouped its advance. If a record goes platinum, this royalty can generate $450,000 to $1 million—not a bad payday for typically a few months' work! In addition, producers receive a pro rata royalty on tracks that may show up on other releases, such as movie soundtracks, compilations, "best of" albums, re-releases, or repackaged albums.

When choosing a producer, listen to his previous work. Is there an identifiable sound to his records? Is there consistency between records? Do you like the arrangements of the songs on these albums? Be sure to talk to other artists who may have worked with the producer you have in mind. Did they feel he added to the project? Was he difficult to work with? Was he amenable to the artist's input or was he stubbornly strong-headed? Did he have any peculiar work habits that might clash with yours? Did the album come in on time and on budget? Would the band work with him again? Ultimately, other artists' input may be the best barometer as you make your decision.

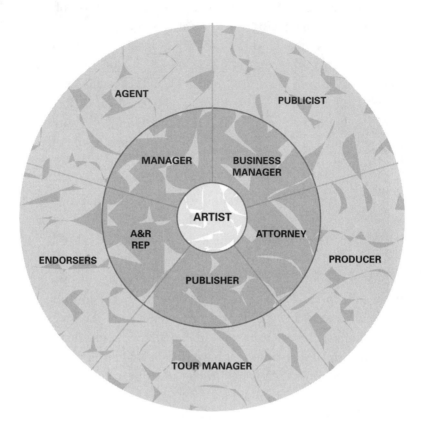

FIGURE 4.1. *A typical major-label recording artist might surround himself with key team members in this fashion. The members of the inner circle—the attorney, the manager, the business manager, the A&R rep, and the publisher—are closer to the artist, as they provide the most important services to the artist and are usually involved on a year-round basis. The outer circle includes the booking agent, the publicist, the producer, endorsers, and the tour manager, who are all very important but are not usually involved with the artist as much as those in the inner circle.*

CHAPTER 5
To Deal or Not To Deal: Publishing, Merchandising, and Endorsements

The decision to make publishing or merchandising deals is one of the most important decisions an artist will ever make. Both publishing and merchandising can provide enormous amounts of income over the course of an artist's career. Merchandising money can be astronomical for a major artist. It is not unusual for a headlining arena act to net half a million dollars per week on the road, and publishing income can continue to generate money long after an artist is retired. As a matter of fact, many writers of the *standards* (famous songs) make more money now than they did when they were performing, as there are more ancillary uses for music now than ever before. Just think of how many times you've heard a popular song in a commercial or in a TV show or movie.

PUBLISHING

There are a lot of different opinions on the topic of publishing arrangements, and there are a lot of things to take into consideration, as publishing itself and the corresponding publishing math is rather complex. Before I explain *what* constitutes publishing revenue and *how* that revenue is obtained, I'll lay out the basics regarding how much of that revenue will reach you, the songwriter.

Music publishing math must be thought of as a "publishing pie" that is composed of two halves: The *publisher's share* and the *writer's share*. Each of these shares is a part of the pie, together totaling 100 percent of the whole pie. Separately, each of these two shares can be divided as well. If you controlled both shares entirely, you would own 100 percent of the publishing pie. If you controlled 100 percent of only the writer's share, you would actually control 50 percent of the whole publishing pie. If you controlled just 50 percent of the writer's share, you would control only 25 percent of the whole publishing pie. When you write a song, you own the publisher's share as well as the writer's share until you assign or sell your interest to another entity. Naturally, if you write songs with someone else, you would own the *portion* of the song that you agreed on. When you control your own publishing (as you do before you assign it to someone else), you will need to start your own publishing company, which will act as a recipient for your writer and publisher royalties. It's not as hard as it sounds; just some paperwork needs to be done with the performing rights society that you will join, and a DBA (Doing Business As) form may need to be filed so you can establish a bank account. Your attorney can assist you with this. Selecting a name for your publishing company can lead to some humorous choices. Check the labels on some of your CDs; you'll see what I mean!

The following charts illustrate the concept of the publishing pie. Figure 5.1 is an example of a full publishing arrangement, whereby the entire publisher's share is assigned to an outside publisher, leaving the writer or writers with 50 percent of the entire pie. Figure 5.2 illustrates a copublishing arrangement, in which only half of the publisher's share is assigned to an outside publisher, giving the writer or writers 75 percent of the overall income.

So, now you know how publishing income is divided and distributed. But just where does all that income come from? It's derived from several sources, and you'd be wise to familiarize yourself with these elements of the business before signing a deal.

Mechanical Income

When a record is sold, it generates a royalty for each song on the album. This is known as *mechanical income.* In the United

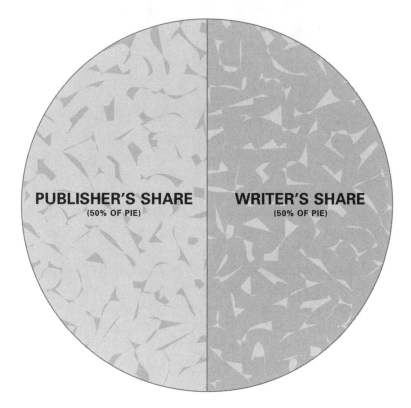

FIGURE 5.1. Full Publishing Deal. *The writer's share occupies 50 percent of the entire pie. If there are multiple band members or other parties involved in the songwriting, the writer's share is divided among these parties according to their partnership agreement—see chapter 2.*

States, there is a set rate known as the *statutory mechanical rate,* which is currently eight cents per song per album. This rate is adjusted from time to time for inflation. This eight-cent figure is an aggregate sum that is divided between the writers and publishers of the song. (Think, *publishing pie!*) Most record companies will pay royalties on a maximum of only ten songs per album (double albums excepted), meaning that the maxi-mum amount the company will pay to the writers and publish-ers for each album sold would be eighty cents. If the record had more than ten songs, then those songs would be prorated on that eighty-cent figure. However, record companies reduce that

FIGURE 5.2. Copublishing Deal. *Here, the writer's share again occupies 50 percent of the entire pie. In addition, the writer(s) have assumed the role of copublisher and therefore are entitled to 50 percent of the publishing share as well. This gives the writer(s) 75 percent of the publishing revenues.*

total amount by enforcing what is known as a *controlled composition* clause, which is, unfortunately, standard in most record contracts. This clause allows the record companies to pay a 3/4 rate on the songs written ("controlled") by the artist. Therefore, if an artist wrote all ten songs on an album, the reduced total mechanical income payable is now sixty cents ($8 \times 10 \times .75$). If the artist recorded twelve songs for the record, the sixty cents are divided by twelve, meaning each song is worth just five cents instead of the original pre-controlled composition clause rate of eight cents. Songs that are not written by the artist are not usually subject to this controlled-composition clause and are paid at full rate to the respective publishers and writers. However, the record company may limit the number of noncontrolled songs it will pay at full rate, and any number beyond this limit may reduce the amount the record company may pay the artist on his own compositions. This gets into some pretty complex math, which is best left for attorneys to negotiate!

Singles are also a significant source of additional mechanical income, and they are paid on the same rate. A hit single can sell 2 million copies or more, over and above the album sales. This could generate upwards of $150,000 for each side of the single. In other countries, the mechanical income is derived by other formulas. For instance, records that are sold in Japan generate a royalty based on a percentage of the wholesale price of the release.

Synchronization Income

If a song is used in a film, a TV show, a multimedia format, or as part of an advertising campaign, a substantial fee may be generated for the writers and publishers of that song. This is known as a *synch* (short for synchronization) *fee.* This fee is an arbitrary amount; there is no set base rate like minimum wage, and it must be negotiated between the user (*licensee*) and the publisher (*licensor*). Negotiators should consider the following factors in determining what that fee may be:

Nature of the Production.
Is this a "B" movie, a major studio motion picture, a network TV show, or a cable show? Is this to be used in a commercial, and, if so, is it local, regional, or national in scope? How long is the campaign? Or is it for nonbroadcast use, such as an in-house corporate video or industrial trade show usage, where there is no profit being generated and no performance income (more on that later) generated?

How the Song Is Used.
Is it a featured part of the movie (like an important love scene or end title) or just a background usage that may

be under dialogue? How much of the song is being used? Is it just a tiny amount (sometimes called a *needledrop*), or is the whole song being used? Will it be used just once in the production, or will there be multiple usages?

What Rights Are Needed for This Usage.
There are a myriad of different *rights* that the licensee may ask for. For example, "Movies of the Week" that may only air on TV in this country may be shown in theaters in Europe or Asia. A *foreign theatrical right* would allow this, and it is a very common option. TV shows may also wind up in videocassette or DVD form in a "best of" collection that may be rented or sold, and, these days, nearly *every* major movie winds up in video stores. (Many "B" movies go straight to video and never show theatrically.) A *videogram buyout* is a fee that is negotiated to allow the production to sell videos that contain your music. It is a one-time fee that may or may not be in the initial quote you negotiate for the usage. You would not be entitled to any additional money if the video sells one copy or one million copies; therefore, you should try to get as big a fee as possible.

The Term Length of the License.
Most times, licensees will ask that the license be granted to them in perpetuity. This way, the licensees are assured that they have the rights forever and don't have to come back to the licensor again for any additional time periods. Normally, licensors charge a premium for this perpetuity term length. However, sometimes in the case of limited-run television shows, the licensee may need only a three- or five-year term initially and will ask for an option to extend it in perpetuity.

Performance Income

Whenever there is a *public performance* of a song, there is a royalty generated by that use that is paid to the writers and publishers of that song. Public performances include usages on radio, TV, and in concerts, or in bars, clubs, malls, and other public places where music is played. As mentioned earlier, there are three major performing rights organizations in the United States that monitor these performances and distribute these royalties: ASCAP, BMI, and SESAC. You can't belong to all three at the same time—you may only join one, as the one you choose would be the *exclusive* representative for you as a writer and would collect on all the material in your catalog. Each society collects millions of dollars each year in license fees from the users of music—major TV networks, cable broadcasters, radio broadcasters, restaurants, malls, health clubs, bars, and even camps! Complex formulas determine the amount that each of the usages generates, and these are computed and distributed on a quarterly basis. Performance income is divided equally between the publisher and the writer of the song. (Think back to that pie that was discussed earlier.)

Television royalties can be very lucrative: A single airing on network television during prime time can generate over $1,500 per song for both the writer and the publisher under the right circumstances. This royalty would be paid *every* time the show aired, so if the show happened to rerun in the same TV season (or go into syndication and play year after year), you could stand to make a *lot* of money. On the radio side, a number one hit song can generate more than $500,000 in radio performances for the writer and the publisher. In the case of BMI, after a song hits the plateau of one million plays, it goes into a bonus payment scale, where each play is worth more. ASCAP and SESAC both have similar bonus structures as well.

Print Royalties

Print royalties are monies that are generated by the sale of physically printed copies of songs. Examples include sheet music of

individual songs, folios (songbooks) such as a matching book to
your record, or compilations such as note-for-note transcrip-
tions. Or perhaps you had a song in a hit movie, and there was
an accompanying book of sheet music from the film.
Arrangements for school marching bands, choruses, or orches-
tras can be extremely lucrative as well.

*Should you decide to do a publishing deal, try to make sure that
the print rights are excluded. This way, you can make a separate deal
for these rights alone.* When I was in Cold Sweat, we negotiated
a separate print deal worth almost $15,000. Fortunately, our
lawyer had excluded the print rights from our publishing contract. Unfortunately, the company decided never to release the
book, but we were paid nonetheless.

Grand Rights

Grand rights are also known as *dramatic performance rights.*
These include the rights to publicly perform compositions in
plays, Broadway shows, ballets, ice shows, and others. Because
these types of shows charge an admission price, they are not
generally considered public performances, even though they are
performed at a public place. Therefore, the three performing
rights organizations would not negotiate or collect on these
rights. In the situation of a Broadway play, the publisher may
negotiate a set fee for the usage of the song, or base the fee on a
percentage of gross receipts from the box office take.

Another example of grand rights would be the use of a song
as the basis for a movie script, where the script would be based
on the lyric of a song, or the song itself would be used so pre-
dominantly in the movie that the movie depended on the song.
In a situation like this, a separate grand right would be negotiated in addition to a synchronization right, and these fees can
range over half a million dollars! There have been several major
motion pictures in recent years that could be used as an example,
most notably *Pretty Woman* (based on the Roy Orbison classic),
Something to Talk About (Bonnie Raitt's hit), *Wild Things,* and
What's Love Got To Do With It (Tina Turner's life story). Again,

as with print rights, the grand rights should be separated from your negotiations with a music publisher, if possible.

Putting It All Together

You now have a general idea of how and where publishing income is derived. It can be complex, but given its extreme importance as perhaps the greatest source of overall income, it is imperative to have some general knowledge about it. I continue to earn publishing income on my old Keel albums from over ten years ago, and I'm earning a good living by licensing songs to film and TV. Figure 5.3 illustrates the various income streams from music publishing.

The Role of the Publisher

Well then, what exactly *does* a publisher do, and why should you consider entering into an agreement with one? When you write a song, you own it in its entirety. Or, if you have two cowriters and have agreed to split everything equally, you would control 33.3 percent of the writer's share and a corresponding 33.3 percent of the publisher's share of that song. For convenience, assume that you wrote all the songs on your album by yourself. You therefore control a 100 percent interest in the album. You are a self-contained publisher at this point, and you would be entitled to 100 percent of all the royalties that the above-mentioned five income streams would generate. Why would you even consider giving up even a portion of these copyrights if they're so valuable and able to generate so much for so long? There are a myriad of factors to take into account when considering a publishing deal with a major publisher. Before we ponder the pros and cons, let's take a look at some of the key functions that publishers perform and how they may affect your decision:

Copyright Administration and Collection of Royalties

Given today's expanding global market, music publishing is a very involved, time-consuming, energy-sapping, work-intensive

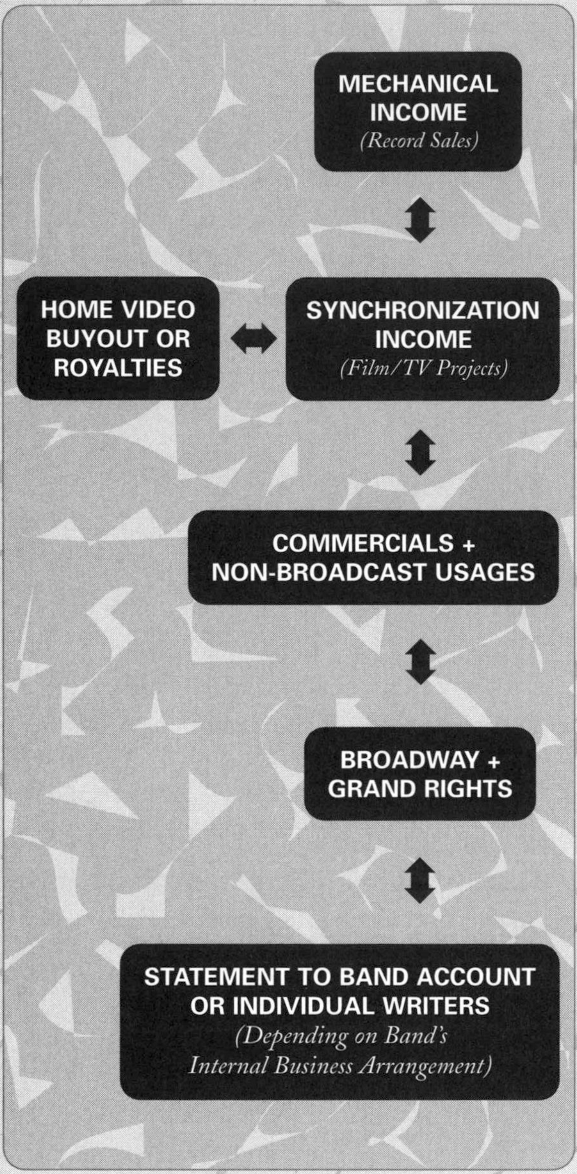

MECHANICAL
INCOME
(Record Sales)

HOME VIDEO
BUYOUT OR
ROYALTIES

SYNCHRONIZATION
INCOME
(Film/TV Projects)

COMMERCIALS +
NON-BROADCAST USAGES

BROADWAY +
GRAND RIGHTS

STATEMENT TO BAND ACCOUNT
OR INDIVIDUAL WRITERS
*(Depending on Band's
Internal Business Arrangement)*

FIGURE 5.3. *Publishing Income Flowchart.*

business. To be even somewhat competent in the field, it requires extensive knowledge of ever-changing copyright and intellectual property law, as well as a background in accounting and entertainment law. Tracking your royalties, ensuring proper payment, and following up on discrepancies can prove to be a legal and logistical nightmare, especially in foreign countries, where language barriers and confusing international law will only add to the workload. All these things are best handled by experienced professionals, as they are well beyond the scope of the average layperson. You are a musical artist—you got into this business because you love *music*. Your time, energy, effort, and passion would be much better directed to creative endeavors such as creating and performing music, not tearing your hair out trying to unbury yourself from an avalanche of administrative tasks.

One of a publisher's key functions is to collect the royalties that are generated throughout the world, account for them, and disperse any payments that may be due you. In the event that someone does not remit the proper amount, your publisher would attempt to rectify the situation, and, if necessary, take legal action to ensure that it happens.

Exploitation of Copyright
Generating uses for songs and therefore adding value to the copyright is another advantage to having a publisher. Getting your songs cut by other artists or placed in major films, TV shows, and commercials is one of the most important services your publisher can perform for you. Generating activity in film or TV is a very specialized part of music publishing that requires specific knowledge of the film and TV industry, the relationships with the licensees of the genre, and the time and ability to service the material. Most major publishers have a film and TV department for just that very reason. Certain themes from hit TV shows, such as "I'll Be There for You" from *Friends,* started out as simply a song on an album but, as a result of a publisher's efforts, went on to become a huge hit on TV, generating hundreds of thousands of dollars in the process.

Having a song on another artist's record (sometimes referred to as a *cut*) can be extremely lucrative. Your album may be a flop, but if another major artist covers one of your songs, he may have a hit on it himself, generating mechanical and performance income for you.

You can write the greatest songs in the world, but if no one hears them, then there's really no value to them beyond the self-serving artistic gratification. A songwriter is like a painter—he creates a work of art. At some point, however, the art has to come out of hiding and into circulation in order for a value to be attached to it. Van Gogh sold but one painting when he was alive; today, his paintings are among the most highly valued pieces in the art world. One role of the publisher is to be the "gallery" of sorts, to "display" this musical art and get it out in circulation, thereby adding commercial value to the copyright.

Advances

When you enter into a publishing or copublishing agreement with a publisher, there is normally an advance payment paid to the writers that is recoupable against future earnings. The amount of the advance is an arbitrary, negotiable figure, determined by a number of different circumstances. Bands on a major label might receive a larger advance because the publisher may feel it has a better opportunity to recoup with a bigger label (bigger label equals bigger push equals more sales). A bidding war or a lot of prerelease hype surrounding the band may also drive the price up for a band's publishing. Or perhaps a member or two of the band have had past success as writers. It is not uncommon for a high-profile, major-label band to get an advance of several hundred thousand dollars.

Very often, this publishing advance can come at a time when the band needs money to keep itself afloat before the record comes out. Bands may also need to invest their own money in independent press or marketing, should the label not cover that, and many times the publishing advance is the only money available. Touring or merchandising money (to be discussed later) may not be available until the band hits the road, which can be months from the time the record is completed.

Cowriting Contacts

Putting you in touch with other writers or members of the creative community is another important service publishers provide. Finding compatible writing partners and stimulating the creative process have helped many writers develop their craft of songwriting, leading to productive results. Most publishers have a stable of writers on their roster, and connecting you with one of these may lead to the formation of a great writing team.

A few years ago, when I was between publishing deals, I visited a friend of mine who worked at MCA Music Publishing. I had sent her a tape of some recent songs I had recorded and was curious about what she thought. While she was not ready to offer me a publishing deal at that time, she gave me the name of a writer who was on the MCA roster with whom she thought I would be compatible. We proceeded to get together, and our first collaboration produced a song called "Kiss the Ground You Walk On." That song has gone on to be in several movies and TV shows and was nearly covered by Curtis Steigers for *The Bodyguard* soundtrack—one of the biggest-selling albums of all time. I had found a great writing partner, and MCA Music Publishing benefited as well from the income generated from these usages.

Promotion

In a publishing or copublishing venture, publishers have a vested interest in the copyright of the songs, as in most cases they have paid an advance to obtain these copyrights. Your publisher wants to recoup on this advance, and selling more copies of a record on which you have songs is certainly one way of doing that. Publishers often will assist the label with marketing and promotional activities or contribute marketing funds to help the band. Sometimes, the publisher may have relationships with various radio promotion people, retail marketers, or members of the print media and may call upon them for certain favors to promote your career. Other times, publishers will take out ads in trade magazines that can help increase the visibility of a young act, helping to begin the hype process that is so critical to a new band.

Publishers often make up compilation *sampler* CDs that include several artists or writers on their roster. These are distributed to the same retail, promotion, and media people and can sometimes be that one "extra thing" that starts the ball rolling. Every little bit helps, and having the muscle of a publisher behind you can only add to your arsenal.

Talking about muscle, I'll give you another example of how our publisher helped our band, going beyond the typical function that publishers provide. When I was in Keel, we were signed to Famous Music, one of the industry's top publishing companies. At that time, Famous Music was owned by Gulf & Western, a huge conglomerate that also owned Madison Square Garden, among other properties. In June 1987, we released our fourth album, called simply *Keel*. Two months prior, I ran into Jon Bon Jovi at a club and told him about our new album. I had known him for several years, and he had always been cordial to me. The next day, we had lunch together and I gave him an advance copy of our album. Fortunately, he liked the album, and suddenly we were in the running to be his support act for the last three weeks of the *Slippery When Wet* tour. Coincidentally, that segment of the tour included three nights at Madison Square Garden. *Un*fortunately, there were a number of bands with higher profiles than Keel that were also up for the slot, and as Bon Jovi's tour was already sold out in advance, they didn't need anyone else's help in selling tickets. We would have to do something special in order for us to beat out those more established bands vying for the coveted opportunity. Having somewhat of a personal relationship with Jon certainly didn't hurt, but it wasn't enough.

When our publisher was informed that we had a shot at the tour (which would potentially add a lot of record sales), it was able to negotiate some reduced rates with the Garden which helped lower the production costs of the tour to the venue. None of the other bands could have done that! We ultimately got the gig and opened up thirteen shows for Bon Jovi, playing the largest indoor venues of our careers. The tour added thousands in sales for us and helped us in more ways than imaginable. Of course, not every publisher is in a position to help like this, but it's a perfect example of how publishers can assist you in some unusual ways.

Structuring the Deal

There are a number of ways a publishing deal can be structured, and because music publishing is a complicated topic, it warrants further study on your part before you sign. There are numerous variables that can figure into the equation, such as the duration, the territories covered, or the scope of material covered (existing songs, future works, or both). There are several great books (see the Resources list) which offer more detailed insights on this topic.

Two of the most popular arrangements are: (1) publishing or copublishing; and (2) administration.

In the standard publishing or copublishing arrangement, the writer "transfers, assigns, sells, or otherwise hereby conveys" the copyright to the publisher. In other words, the writer is assigning a part of the ownership of the song to the publisher. Again, the duration of this assignment can be negotiated, and at the end of such a term, the copyrights can revert back to the writer. In a *full* publishing scenario, the publisher will own 100 percent of the publisher's share of the pie, and in a *copublishing* venture, the publisher owns 50 percent of that pie, with writers owning the remainder.

These days, copublishing deals are more the norm than full publishing deals. In earlier times in the music industry, artists were not in the same position of leverage as they are today, given the enormous amount of income that now derives from publishing. Remember: Copublishing deals give the artist more ownership and a larger portion of the earning pie. However, if you are in a position of being offered either a full publishing deal or nothing at all, you may not be in a position to negotiate.

An *administrator,* on the other hand, does not own the copyrights to your songs. He does, however, perform a lot of the same administrative functions as a publisher, such as collecting monies, preparing copyright forms and renewals, or issuing synch licenses to film and TV. Administrators normally charge a percentage for their work, ranging from 10 percent to 25 percent. Some music lawyers also perform these same tasks and may charge an hourly rate for their services instead of a percentage. *Admin* (industry jargon for "administrative") deals may also offer an advance. However, there is not the same incentive for administrators to pitch your material, as they do not share in the ownership of it. Additionally, some administrators do not have the full staff necessary for the proper exploitation of your copyrights.

Pros and Cons of Publishing Deals

Publishing is often the most lucrative and longest-lasting source of income in the music business. Given the complexity of publishing and the monetary ramifications involved, this is a decision that must be clearly weighed and thought out. It is my opinion that major publishers have a lot of benefits to offer artists, especially newer ones, and that the "pros" outweigh the "cons." Don't forget: The publisher is taking somewhat of a gamble on you, too. No one knows for sure how many records you will sell. If you get a large publishing advance, and your album stiffs, your publisher is out that money. There have been instances in which a publisher has given an artist an advance, and then the album never came out! Most times, the artist gets to keep this money, and the publisher is left out in the cold. Certainly this is a "pro" in the artist's favor. And again, a good publisher will have a variety of ways to generate income for you beyond that which might be generated solely from your record sales.

However, signing a publishing deal is not for everyone. Some writers take the position of wanting to own their works entirely in perpetuity, and they want to maintain absolute control over their copyright's destiny. Some writers have an aversion to commercial usage of their songs and feel that their songs are pure art and shouldn't be associated with corporations or certain products. Once a publisher acquires the copyright, it can allow your song to be used in such commercial ventures, sometimes without your approval, depending on your contract.

If you're an established, multiplatinum artist who consistently sells a lot of records and doesn't need any ancillary income, giving up a portion of your publishing may not be the best financial move for you to make, as you'd be giving up 25 percent of your income with a standard copublishing arrangement. An administration deal would be better suited to artists of this stature.

Perhaps you've got a feeling that several years down the road, you're going to be huge. If you can get by without that publisher's advance (the label will pay you your publisher's share and your writer's share in its normal accounting periods), it may be a better move to cash in your chips later, when you're the big star you hope to be. In any event, be sure to get advice from trusted people, whether your manager, attorney, or other confidant, and go in making a knowledgeable decision.

MERCHANDISING DEALS

Merchandising is what the name implies: It is the selling of merchandise. In this case the product is not music, but rather items that carry the name, likeness, album artwork, or related images of an artist. Merchandising money can be absolutely astronomical. In the short term, it can far exceed monies brought in by record sales or even publishing. Many bands sell marginal amounts of records but clean up on the road with merchandising. The business of licensing the name, likeness, or other products can extend beyond the realm of the typical fare found at concerts, such as T-shirts, hats, program books, and pins. The group KISS is a perfect example of this: They've licensed items such as lunch boxes, video games, makeup kits, and even coffins!

Merchandising income can be a substantial revenue source long after an artist has retired from the stage, or even after his death. Elvis Presley's estate brings in an estimated $100 million per year, a good percentage of which is derived from licensed merchandise. Many popular bands from the 1970s that have since broken up are still selling millions of dollars per year in merchandise.

A merchandising company manufactures the various band products and then sells that product at the band's live dates. It sends a crew along with the band's touring entourage that sets up display booths in the venues and sells the product during the concerts. The venue normally receives a percentage of the merchandise receipts (sometimes called the *take*.) This percentage normally ranges between 25 percent and 40 per-cent and can actually be higher than the commission a band will receive on each sale, which normally ranges from 20 per-cent to 35 percent. This is the major reason that merchandise has become so expensive. It has always seemed unfair to me that venues charge this commission to merchandisers—they make plenty from the rental fee charged to the promoters, the parking, and concessions. Unfortunately, this commission is passed on to the consumer in the form of higher merchandise prices.

The merchandise company is responsible for an accurate accounting of each night's take, the dispersal to the venue, and the remittance back to the band. The band usually gets an advance prior to the tour; however, if the merchandising compa-ny recoups this advance while on the road, the band may elect to take the additional earnings while on the road to help finance the tour or use for miscellaneous expenses.

An industry term called *per head* is used as a gauge to deter-mine how much is spent by an audience on any given night. The gross receipts are divided by the attendance, and the resulting figure is the average amount each person in the crowd spends on merchandising. An average figure would be anywhere from $7 to $10 per head. In other words, if you were playing at a club that had a crowd of four hundred, and the merchandise take was $4,000, the *per head* would be $10 that particular night—a very good average. With very popular bands that headline arenas, it is not uncommon to have per head counts of $15 to $18. When you start drawing 15,000 to 18,000 people every night, you can bring in $200,000 nightly! Over the course of a major tour that may last for one hundred dates, a cumulative total may approach $20 million. Just imagine the kind of money world-class bands like the Rolling Stones, U2, Aerosmith, or KISS can earn. It's amazing!

In addition to monies earned at live concerts, merchandise can also be sold through retail outlets and mail-order houses. Merchandise can thus be sold in rural places that a band may not be scheduled to play in or allow people who missed the concert to purchase token items emblazoned with the name or logo of their favorite band. Some bands have merchandise information and order forms in their albums, allowing their fans the ability to purchase items immediately, usually through a toll-free number.

As opposed to publishing, where there may be valid reasons not to enter into an arrangement with a publishing company, there really aren't *any* reasons *not* to do a merchandising deal. It's more a question of finding the right company and negotiating the best deal possible with the largest advance and the best terms. If you don't do a merchandise deal at all (and therefore do not have any merchandise available), you are committing financial suicide by depriving yourself of a *huge* source of income—perhaps the biggest windfall of all. Don't forget: Merchandise money is not correlated to the performance of your record, as is mechanical income and publishing income. You may have unrecouped advances from your label to the tune of hundreds of thousands of dollars, yet become millionaires from T-shirt sales!

OWN YOUR OWN GRAPHICS!

One very important issue relating to this topic: It is *imperative* that you own your own logo; otherwise, you may have to license it from the owner (such as the label or independent graphic artist) just to use it. If the label's art department designs your logo, be sure it's stated in your record contract that *you* own the logo, not them. The same goes for album artwork. Many times, the label's own art department will design your album artwork, which is one of the most popular forms of merchandise graphics because it has a built-in recognition factor with the fans. If it is not specifically stated in your record contract, you may have to pay a fee to the label for permission to use this artwork. Likewise, if you hire an outside artist to do the design, *make sure* you draft and both sign an agreement stating that *you* own the logo and album art and are free and clear to license it in any form without any future payments to the graphic artist. I have heard of many bands that were prevented from using their own album artwork or were forced to pay exorbitant fees to graphic artists because of this. This work should be done on a *work-for-hire* basis, and *you* should own all the rights to it.

ENDORSEMENT DEALS

Endorsements can be a very powerful ally to an artist, providing support on many different levels. In a typical endorsement deal, the artist receives free goods or services in exchange for the use of his name or likeness in promoting these goods or services. For a band that's just beginning its career, getting free musical gear is like manna from heaven. Many times, an up-and-coming artist may not have a lot of discretionary income to afford the latest equipment. Therefore, an endorsement deal can be just what the doctor ordered. In addition, the endorsee may benefit from advertisements that appear in various publications. These ads can be extremely beneficial by increasing the visibility of the artist and may also be coordinated with the artist's touring schedule, helping increase the awareness of the tour. Some endorsement deals may even include a cash or equity arrangement for the artist, although these types of deals are normally reserved for more established, popular artists. Additionally, the artist may even get his own line of equipment and receive a royalty for each unit sold.

When I was in Keel, I was fortunate to be able to be involved with some great companies. My first endorsement was with Charvel/Jackson, who was one of the premier guitar makers at that time. I got to appear in several of the company's national ad campaigns, and Charvel/Jackson gave me several handmade guitars built to my exact specifications. Later, I secured a deal with Peavey, who provided me with several top-of-the-line amplifiers and a wall of speaker cabinets. I even designed my own guitar with company designers, and Peavey incorporated a cosmetic design of mine on the company's line of electric guitars—I even got it patented!

Another company that was very helpful to me in a number of ways was St. Louis Music, the parent company of Ampeg, Crate, and Alvarez. In addition to providing me with some of the finest acoustic guitars and amplifiers on the market, the company was very helpful to my career by including me in its catalogs and print advertising campaigns. St. Louis Music's artist relations person, Ken Hensley, was himself a professional musician (keyboardist for Uriah Heep) and understood the importance of the symbiotic affiliation between endorser and endorsee. He was very instrumental in helping to cultivate the relationship that proved to be mutually beneficial to both parties. I became a touring clinician for the company, giving product demonstrations all over the United States over the course of several years. This helped me both on a financial level and on a publicity level by keeping my name in contact with the public. I got to meet some great people on these clinic tours, and it was one of the most rewarding experiences of my career.

Other endorsements I had were with La Bella (guitar strings), GHS (guitar strings), Pro-Co (cables and distortion pedals), DigiTech (special effects), and Performance Guitars. On the nonmusical side, I had endorsement deals with a sunglass company, a local hair salon, and even Adidas!

Bear in mind that you may have to sign a contract with the company that may bind you for a specific period of time or limit you to the types of other endorsements that you may enter into. You may even be obligated to return whatever goods that were given to you if you do not fulfill your obligations. Therefore, when deciding on an endorsement deal, you should ask yourself a few key questions before jumping in: Do you honestly believe in the product? Do you intend to actually use the product? Will you have any regrets about this in the future? Will your association with this company reflect on you in a negative way? Will you be in elite company with other artists of your stature?

Your image, reputation, and goodwill are precious commodities, which may not recover from a tarnished relationship.

CHAPTER 6

Taking It to the Streets: Perils, Potholes, and Pitfalls of the Road

For thousands of years, musicians have been taking their act on the road. From the ancient wandering minstrels to the latest arena rock tours, music has always been about playing live. Although it's certainly enjoyable listening to music on records, the real energy and passion shines through when there are 5,000 watts of power and raw human emotion driving it. Most musicians will tell you that there is nothing in the world like the feeling you get playing in front of a live audience. The bigger the crowd, the more energy it feeds to you. It's like a huge wave—it holds awesome power, and if you catch it just right, you can harness it and tap into it like an electric socket energizing your soul. Some liken this feeling to that of sex or empowerment, others to a runner's high or a rush. I think it's greater than any of these things because you are feeding off the collective energies of thousands of souls and using this energy to give back to these same souls by virtue of your performance. It's no wonder that performers often change personalities once on stage or develop alter egos; it is easy to become seduced by this power and get addicted to it.

Being on the road is like being in the circus, the Army, and the insane asylum all at the same time. It's a twenty-four-hour-a-day adventure that never seems to have a beginning or an end. Sometimes road trips are organized with military precision; other times they are painted by utter chaos. It's exhilarating and exhausting at the same time, an experience that every performing musician should have the opportunity to have.

The World Tour!
Photo credit: Marc Ferrari.

When things are going well, touring can be the best working vacation you could ever have—you're seeing the world,
meeting new people, experiencing new cultures, playing for
appreciative audiences, and making money. When things are
bad, a day on the road can seem like hell. Being sick or lonely,
playing for hostile crowds, and having bad organization and
long, grueling travel schedules can all contribute to making a
tour seem like a prison sentence.

Everything tends to get magnified on the road. You become
"married" to the guys in the band and crew, and spending long
periods of time with people in close quarters can stretch one's

tolerance of others to the breaking point. Everyone's annoying habits, personality flaws, and irritating traits get blended together, and the outcome can be an explosive mix, like putting a match to a tank of gas. People who are normally calm, reserved, and rational have snapped and become raving lunatics, stressed to their limit like a Jekyll and Hyde complex. It's easy to see why most arguments and band breakups occur on the road—the whole thing can become like a compression chamber, and the tiniest spark can set it all off.

Most people assume that being on the road is all glamour: first-class travel, four-star accommodations, fine food, and pampering adulation. They see their favorite star on stage for those few brief moments and think that he has it made. His whole day is probably spent lounging by a pool, his entourage at his feet. He feasts on the finest foods available. His every wish and whim is magically fulfilled. He is driven by chauffeured limousine to the venue, where he steps on stage to tantalize his screaming fans. He may play for two hours or less, then he's whisked away to some other locale, only to repeat the same routine again.

With Steven Tyler, opening up for Aerosmith.
Photo credit: Marc Ferrari.

This, of course, is mostly fantasy. For the majority of musicians who go on the road, the hypothetical scenario above is merely a dream sequence that will never be realized. Reality is a far, far different scenario without any of the so-called glamour. Sure, headline arena acts may only play for one to two-and-a-half hours a night (opening acts play even less—sometimes for as little as thirty minutes). However, the daily process of just getting to that short time on stage can involve nearly the remaining twenty-two or so hours of the day. It is often a monotonous, arduous grind that can wear out even the most vigorous person.

PUTTING TOGETHER YOUR ROAD TEAM

Surrounding yourself with a competent crew is very important in ensuring a smooth operation. Here's a look at several important people who make up the core of the touring regimen.

Tour Manager

The tour manager is the most important piece of the puzzle when it comes to touring. A competent tour manager can make the difference between a good tour and a great one. Part business liaison, part father figure, part sheriff, part psychiatrist, the tour manager's responsibilities are far-reaching and almost never-ending. He is usually the person who spends the most time with the band and has the closest rapport with each member, as his responsibilities entail so many different functions. His duties typically include *advancing* the dates with the promoter (ensuring that everything is going smoothly), coordinating the band's personal scheduling for interviews or public appearances, taking care of the guest list for each night, accommodating those guests at the venues, arranging for the hotels and check-ins, collecting the money from the promoter, distributing weekly salaries or per diems (if there is no tour accountant), communicating between the band management and the booking agent, and acting as liaison between the band and local radio, press, or label representatives. When intraband squabbles escalate into fistfights, the tour manager often acts as a mediator. When certain band members wind up in the local jail, the trustworthy tour manager can normally be found coming to the rescue! When other emergencies arise, the tour manager is there, putting out the fires. In short, the role of a tour manager is all-encompassing!

Production Manager

The production manager is in charge of coordinating the actual moving pieces of the tour. Prior to the beginning of the tour, he may hire the entire road crew, including trucking companies, sound and light companies, special effects or pyrotechnic specialists, individual technicians for specialized jobs, local or foreign cargo coordinators, and others. He acts as an intermediary between the band's crew and local unions, since the unions are required to load in and pack out gear in any union facility. He thoroughly plans the stage show, ensuring that the dimensions of the stage will fit in all venues in the tour. If there are local fire ordinances regarding stage explosions or lasers, he coordinates with proper authorities in each city. If the tour includes foreign territories, it would be his responsibility to ensure proper electrical needs for the show, as voltage differs from country to country. While on the road, he is the "captain of the ship" and takes on a role not unlike a drill sergeant. He oversees the entire operation and makes sure everyone is pulling their share of the weight, both on an individual basis and as part of the overall team.

Sound Person, Monitor Person, and Light Person

These jobs fall under the heading of *production*. With bigger tours, separate companies may be hired for house sound, monitors, and lighting. Each of these companies provides its own crew for the tour, and they are contracted out at a negotiated fee. These crews rehearse with the band for a specified period in order to learn the songs better and to make for a stronger show.

It is not uncommon, however, for bigger bands to have their own sound, monitor, and light persons on salary as their own permanent employees. This way, they are certainly much more familiar with the band and their material than any outside vendor could be, and when the band is off the road, they may become part of the office staff. Smaller bands that are not headlining will normally bring one person on tour for each of these positions, and they may also have crossover responsibilities, such as loading the equipment, changing guitar strings, or driving a truck. Of course, the opening bands don't get to use all the power or lights that the headlining band does, and sometimes the opening band's crew has to be supervised by the headliner's. This can lead to some strained relationships, which, as I have witnessed on more than one occasion, can result in outright physical confrontations.

Tour Accountant

On big headline tours, enormous amounts of money are generated on a nightly basis. The band is usually paid 50 percent up front before the tour for each venue, with the remaining balance paid at the end of the night's performance. For a major-status headline band, this may be in the hundreds of thousands of dollars, with some or all of it in cash. If the band has its own merchandising, this figure may be doubled. With the sheer madness of being on the road, and with the volume of money coming in on a daily basis, it's easy to see how money may somehow get lost or be unaccounted for. A tour accountant is responsible for ensuring that all monies are collected, properly accounted for, and deposited. He may also be responsible for dispersing weekly salaries, *per diems* (daily allowances for food or incidental items), cash floats (advances), and other miscellaneous expenditures.

When bands play in foreign countries, the whole issue of converting currency and paying any local or government taxes can become a nightmare. Here is where it is imperative to have an expert in international business law, as this can become a very intricate and involved matter. Many times the tour accountant is from the same office as the band's business manager, and this helps with the overall accounting process. At the conclusion of the tour, the tour accountant would coordinate all income and expenses with the business management, provide 1099s and other tax-related documents, and generate the tour-end reports and analysis.

A TYPICAL DAY IN THE LIFE

First of all, there is no such thing as "typical" on the road. Although each day may bring about some of the same repetitive activities, every day presents itself with a different set of unique circumstances. It's like going on a slightly different, but semi-similar, adventure every day; you never quite know entirely what's in store for you. Secondly, touring is a twenty-four-hour-a-day process that makes it difficult to pinpoint where one "day" ends and the next one starts. Days overlap into each other and become a blur. You begin to lose feel for what your reality is. You have no reference point, as you would if you were living at your own home, going to the same job and seeing the same group of people every day. On the road, you have no anchor to hold on to, no clock to set your watch by. Towns begin to look the same, hotels begin to look like carbon copies of each other, venues look identical, food starts tasting all too familiar, and each crowd looks like the one you just saw the previous night. It's no wonder some performers have to be reminded every night which town they're playing in. Many times, the band is in town for less than a twenty-four-hour period, arriving just in time for the gig and leaving shortly thereafter.

Support bands are usually on stage for just forty-five minutes, sometimes as few as thirty minutes if it's a three-band bill. Headliners normally get a minimum of ninety minutes. Generally, they're *contracted* for a minimum of ninety minutes but may play longer. Led Zeppelin used to play three-and-a-half-hour concerts, but they tended not to have any support bands, therefore avoiding union overtime penalties. As most

U.S. concert venues are sanctioned union halls, the union has strict guidelines on the hours each union member can work. If concerts go into overtime, it winds up costing the promoter a lot of money in overtime payments, so most shows finish at a predetermined time. If a headline band goes into overtime, the additional union fees incurred can be charged back to them, depending on their contract with the promoter.

A quasi-average twenty-four-hour period for a support band on the road might go something like this, taking into consideration that the day started with the time on stage, and that there was a travel day to the next venue. For liberty's sake we will also assume that the band is traveling in a tour bus.

8:00 P.M.–8:45 P.M. On stage.

8:45 P.M.–9:15 P.M. Shower (if possible); prepare for onslaught of well-wishers.

9:15 P.M.–11:00 P.M. Post-gig interviews; meet and greet local radio personnel, contest winners, record company reps, etc. Find the babes from the front row; start a fifteen-minute relationship. Road crew loads gear into truck. Tour manager or accountant settles with promoter, gets paid.

11:00 P.M.–12:00 A.M. Band and crew leave for next venue. Visit local greasy spoon for late night munchies.

12:00 A.M.–2:00 A.M. Unwind on bus, listen to evening's performance. If in a van instead, drive on to next venue in silence, trying to get a few hours of sleep with five other guys on top of each other, trying to ignore each other's various body emittances.

2:00 A.M.–8:00 A.M. Travel to next town. Sleep?

8:00 A.M.–10:00 A.M. Arrive in next town, check into hotel, or stay on bus. Quality sleep time!

10:00 A.M.–11:00 A.M. Wake up; breakfast.

11:00 A.M.–2:00 P.M. Free time: Do laundry, visit local music store for supplies, find post office, give prearranged phone interviews, call manager or girlfriend, etc.

2:00 P.M.–5:00 P.M. Visit local radio station for on-air interviews, make in-store appearances, conduct autograph sessions at record stores, give local television or newspaper interviews. Local record company representative arranges transportation.

5:00 P.M.–6:30 P.M. Sound check at venue, followed by dinner.

6:30 P.M.–8:00 P.M. Back to hotel for shower or, if no hotel, stay at venue until show time.

8:00 P.M.– . . . Repeat steps 1–12.

A day off is one of the rarest commodities in touring life. Many times, a whole day is necessary just to get from one town to the next, so the term "day off" is quite misleading. However, if there is that exception where a date is canceled and you find yourself in a town the day before your next scheduled performance, a day off is truly a blessing. It is in these rare times that you can catch up on sleep, finish that new song you're working on, go see that movie you've been wanting to see, see an old friend who lives nearby, or explore the town a little bit.

Ah, the road! You've heard or imagined all the stories. Some revolve around sexual escapades, others around comic episodes or unusual circumstances. Let's face it: A lot of so-called musicians decide to get into music for such fringe benefits as groupies, drugs, adulation, or being part of the scene. The music part of it sometimes tends to be the secondary reason for everything. It certainly wasn't that way in my case, but I know for a fact it is with some of my peers.

SEX AND DRUGS ON THE ROAD

Now, I'm not going to sit here and tell you I was an angel when I was on the road and didn't experience firsthand the kinds of things that went on all around me. On the contrary, I was a willing participant. I may not have indulged in all the excesses that others did, but I certainly got my feet wet, as the saying goes. When you're young, naïve, and full of curiosity and hormones, things happen—that's just a fact of life. On the road, anything and everything happens. The girls want to hang out with the band, and guys want to become your friends, and they are usually the ones showing up with drugs or alcohol. There's an old saying: "If you invite trouble, it is usually eager to accept." If you're looking for drugs, they're always around. Wanna get laid? It's as easy as waking up. Of course, these relationships are fleeting, and they're hardly ever meaningful. These days, they can be deadly. The onslaught of AIDS has put a lot of touring musicians in a reduced-contact mode, but it certainly isn't stopping everyone. I feel extremely fortunate that I escaped that part of my life unscathed and in perfect health—a lot of close friends didn't.

I was never that popular with girls. I came from a small agricultural town, and all the girls gravitated toward the jocks in high school. Even though I was in a popular band with our own self-proclaimed fan club, the girls all thought I was "cute" rather than sexy. They all just wanted to be my friend. I wasn't with a girl until I was almost nineteen—I was beginning to think it was never gonna happen! When I moved to Boston, it got a little better for me. I actually had two steady girlfriends in the three years I lived there, even though longhaired rocker guys were not the preferred type of guy in that part of the country.

When I moved out to Los Angeles, everything just exploded. The rock scene was in full bloom. Groupies and strippers were everywhere. These girls *loved* musicians, and if you had long hair, you were "in like Flynn"! Everyone wants to feel wanted; it was a new experience for me to have girls want me. If you're thirsty, you drink. Well, for those first months in L.A., I could've drowned.

Going on the road magnifies everything even more. In any given town there'd be several girls vying for the guys in the band. Granted, they may not have wanted me for *who* I was (the real me), but for *what* I was. That's the whole thing about being on the road and meeting new people for the first time. Everyone has an agenda, an ulterior motive. Everyone wants a piece of you, like a souvenir. Girls want to sleep with you because it's a conquest for them, and guys want to hang out with you to feel important.

Trying to keep a level head about sex on the road can be a difficult task. Having great-looking girls throw themselves at you is a temptation that can be hard to resist. You're far from home, lonely, and wanting companionship, and hormones are raging. Finding temporary solace in a stranger is a solution for some, but after a while, it starts to feel hollow. If you haven't been on the road, it's difficult to understand. If you've ever cheated on someone and felt guilty about it, you'd have an idea—then multiply it by ten. Even though many musicians have met their future wives (and ex-wives) on the road, I haven't kept in touch with a single person I met in all those years of touring. It just goes to show you: Those temporary liaisons didn't add up to a thing. But, hey, *to each his own.*

The drug thing wasn't a big issue for me. Like most other people my age, I experimented with it. Pot made me groggy, so I could never smoke during the day; I'd just become slow, sloppy, and silly. The only time I'd smoke would be late at night to get to sleep. Coke made me jumpy, and, besides, I couldn't afford it! It was always around, and I used it occasionally, but it wasn't my stimulant of choice. I hated speed—I was uptight and energetic enough without it. Apart from my escapade with Valium back in my Boston days, I never ventured into harder drugs, like prescription drugs or heroin. I had already seen what those could do to other musicians and wasn't interested in becoming another statistic. I drank a fair amount but was fortunate enough not to develop a dependency on alcohol. Look, I'm not here to preach to anyone about how to behave on the road.

I wasn't exactly the poster boy for the "healthy and moral lifestyle" campaign. I lived out a lot of fantasies. I did what I did. I'm not proud of a lot of the things that happened, but they're all life experiences that, for better or worse, have made up a part of me. In a nutshell: On the road, anything goes. If you're looking for something, whatever it is, you'll find it. Just know that there are consequences to every action. Some consequences can't be reversed.

PICKING THE RIGHT ALIAS

One of the most endearing traditions of being on the road is coming up with a creative name to use as an alias. Using an alias can reduce the number of unwanted phone calls or distractions and can help protect your privacy. It may even help as a security measure, too. Although most celebrity-seekers are well-meaning and not a security threat, there are enough weirdos and wackos in the world to warrant a little blanketing from the general populace. John Lennon's brutal murder is a testament to that. Some take another famous person's name or a sports figure; others come up with their own monikers. A few more famous road names have included:

Ivan Awfulich	*Al Kaholl*
Harry Balczyk	*Dick Long*
Seymour Bush	*Willy Makitt*
Will Call	*Jack Meoff*
Justin Case	*Guy Nicologist*
Ben Dover	*Nick O'Tyme*
Dick Gozinya	*Pete Serria*
Kenny Holdett	*Allen Wrench*
Hugh Jorgan	

And for you ladies out there, a few apply to the female side:

Terry Cloth	*Helena Handbag*
Betty Dozer	*Anita Mann*
Ida Dunham	*Carrie Oki*
Barb Dwyer	*Anne Phetamine*

For many years I registered under Reuben Kincaid, who in TV life was the manager of the Partridge Family. I thought it was quite appropriate, given the nature of our band!

Hotels tend to be gathering sites for after-show parties. Hotel security is normally much less stringent than that found at the venues, and oftentimes hotels have bars or lounges where the band, crew, and fans can congregate. The huge tour buses are usually a dead giveaway as to where the band is staying, so opportunistic well-wishers can usually figure out just where the mob will be gathering!

By the way, bear in mind that if you plan to use your hotel room as party central, you will be obligated to pay any damages incurred. Many groups have found themselves banned from various hotel chains because they trashed their rooms and then skipped town without paying for the damages.

Opening up for Van Halen in front of 80,000 people!
Photo credit: Marc Ferrari.

ROAD STORIES

Keel had the good fortune of going on tour in Europe in the
spring of 1986. Our travels took us to Finland, Norway, Sweden,
Denmark, Germany, Holland, Belgium, France, Scotland, and
England over the course of six weeks. It was my first visit to
many of these places, and it was the first time any of us had the
chance to play for audiences outside our native U.S.A. One
would think that we would have been able to take in some of
the famous sights of these wonderful places, but in actuality we
had very little time to do what normal tourists would do, due to
our demanding schedule. We wound up seeing the Eiffel Tower
for ten minutes on our way out of town after our show. I saw
Big Ben and the Tower of London from a taxicab on my way to
a show. I might have had four or five days off the whole time,
which I spent mostly in laundromats. And, thanks to perfect
timing, we spent a good part of our trip fearing terrorism from
Libya and nuclear fallout from Russia—we'd managed to choose
six weeks that would overlap with the U.S. bombing of Libya
(in response to the terrorist seizure of the cruise ship Achille
Lauro in the Mediterranean, and the killing of several
American passengers) and the tragic meltdown at Chernobyl.

The Eiffel Tower.
Photo credit: Marc Ferrari.

Making friends with fans in Europe.
Photo credit: Marc Ferrari.

Japan proved to be an amazing experience. In Japan, artists are treated with reverence and respect, the likes of which is not seen in the Western Hemisphere. The fans are fiercely loyal and extremely generous, and it is a custom for them to give gifts. They devour all information about bands and their pasts. It was amazing that many knew about my cover band from Boston—how did they even dig up that information? From the moment we landed, we knew it was going to be an amazing time. There were nearly two hundred girls at the airport waving signs, banners, posters, and the like, many bearing gifts or flowers. They waited for us to clear customs, and as soon as we made it past the gates, they all descended on us like a scene out of *Beatlemania*. Although they were individually very polite and well-meaning, as a group together it was a little daunting, because they were all pushing and screaming at the same time. I had never experienced that kind of adulation before, and at first it was uncomfortable. The whole pack moved together, and many from this group proceeded to follow us for the next eight days, even traveling to Osaka and Nagoya.

A warm welcome in Japan.
Photo credit: Marc Ferrari.

One day, the promoter's staff took us shopping in Tokyo. We all piled into a cab. About ten girls proceeded to get into another couple of cabs behind us. Now, the staff guys knew these girls, and were tired of them following us around all the time. All the cabs took off at the same time. About a quarter-mile down the road, the staff guy had our cab pull over. The other two cabs followed suit. He got out of the car, walked behind to the two other cab drivers, and proceeded to pay them off to dump the girls! The girls were so devastated they began to cry. We all thought it was hilarious, like a scene out of a Marx Brothers movie. Of course, we felt bad for the girls and everything, but the way it happened was so funny. They were waiting for us when we returned from shopping anyway.

In Japan, there is little violent crime to speak of. People leave their car doors unlocked, and the streets and sidewalks are spotless. We were able to escape the road on occasion, stopping by Kiddyland, the world's largest toy store, with five huge floors filled with every conceivable type of toy from old collectibles to board games, to the newest electronic gizmos found only in Japan. We ate excellent food, rode the Bullet Train, visited geisha houses, and benefited tremendously from the generosity of the people—by the time we left, we had been given so many gifts that we had to have special boxes shipped back along with our music gear. The hospitality of the Japanese people never ceases to amaze me—I wish everyone could be like that.

Back in the good ol' U.S.A., we've had some pretty interesting experiences as well. A few have been out-and-out hilarious, like a scene from *This Is Spinal Tap*. For those of you who don't know what *Spinal Tap* is, it's a movie about a British rock band that goes on tour in the United States, and everything that could possibly go wrong does. It was directed by Rob Reiner and came out in 1984. The main cast of Michael McKean, Christopher Guest, and Harry Shearer is hilarious, and a lot of now-famous actors such as Billy Crystal, Fran Drescher, Dana Carvey, and Bruno Kirby make cameo appearances. Some famous musicians who appear include Paul Shaffer (the

Meeting new people!
Photo credit: Marc Ferrari.

Ron Keel and I in Tokyo with a poster for our show.
Photo credit: Marc Ferrari.

bandleader on *The Late Show with David Letterman*), Cherie Currie from the Runaways, Paul Shortino from Rough Cutt, and Blackie Lawless from W.A.S.P. The movie is so funny it will make you hurt from laughing so much. The term *Spinal Tap* has now become synonymous with real-life events that befall bands on the road, such as showing up in the wrong town for a show or being a day late for a gig. (It's happened to more than one group I know of!) Well, we've had our own share of *Spinal Tap*–type events!

On our first tour, we were traveling in a motor home. We couldn't afford a big tour bus yet, and had a total of five band members and five crew members—too many for a van. So a motor home seemed like the perfect choice. As there weren't enough bunks or couches for everyone, we bought foam padding and made beds on the floor. Well, the bathroom over-flowed one night, and the guys on the floor woke up smelling pretty ripe, to say the least. That's one for the *Spinal Tap* books, but even funnier was the time we got stuck underneath a bridge on our way to a record-store signing.

This particular motor home had an air conditioning unit that stuck up from the top about two feet. Unfortunately, no one had factored these additional two feet into the overall height of the motor home, because it was an add-on unit. One day, we were running late to an in-store appearance and, to save time, took a shortcut that a local had told us about. Well, wouldn't you know that this particular shortcut passed under a low, one-lane bridge made of stone. The warning sign said the clearance for the bridge was thirteen feet, and we knew the truck wasn't that tall. Of course, we hadn't figured for the air conditioning unit. What we also didn't know was that the bridge was slightly lower on the far side. As we approached the bridge, we knew we were going to be close, so we took it real slow—about five miles an hour. About halfway through, we heard the scraping. Then a big "thunk." We all got out to investigate. We had lodged the motor home right into the bridge! Going in reverse, we tried to back out, but the air conditioning unit was starting to break away from the rest of the truck. Well, between us ten geniuses, we came up with the idea to let some air out of the tires and back out. It worked, but of course we now had flat tires. We had to call the store and get rides over. So much for a graceful entrance!

One of the classic scenes in *Spinal Tap* is when the band arrives at a gig only to find out from the marquee that they're second-billed to a puppet show. After headlining arenas, they had a downward spiral and had been relegated to secondary markets with a more "selective audience"! Well, I've got one even better. By 1986, Keel had attained a certain level of popularity and had begun to actually headline shows in some cities. We may have been more popular in certain cities due to local radio stations playing our music or the local press getting behind the band. Milwaukee was one of these cities, and we were excited to be headlining there for the first time. Normally, we would play in clubs where there would be an over-eighteen (or twenty-one) ordinance, but this promoter wanted to have an all-ages show. The only venue he could find was a ballroom that belonged to the Eagles, a fraternal organization similar to the Kiwanis, Rotary, or the Lions Club.

The venue was a big-sized building, with halls on three different levels, allowing several functions to be held at the same time. What the promoter hadn't told us was that the Eagles had a function there at the same time, underneath ours! When we arrived at the venue, the marquee proclaimed in huge letters, "FRIDAY NIGHT: FISH FRY," and in the smallest letters possible: "Also, Keel." We were outbilled by a damn dinner! At least *Spinal Tap* got second billing to a theatrical act of some type! To make matters worse, the Eagles threw a fit as soon as we started playing. I guess the promoter hadn't told them that we weren't exactly an easy-listening cover band. The cops came out, making it a nuisance for everyone, particularly our group. I did extract some kind of revenge by getting very friendly with the daughter of the police chief. She was a lot more accommodating than her father, to say the least. I always enjoyed playing Milwaukee. The next time, we even got top billing!

Girls—a strange, intriguing, beguiling, intoxicating, beautiful life-form, they. Think a lot about 'em, write songs about 'em, get tongue-tied over 'em, and get into trouble over 'em. Many a comical moment has ensued in the pursuit of girls. I say "comical" because I tend to get awkward and goofy around girls, being the introvert I am. I've made a fool of myself more times than I care to admit. Girls can do some silly things as well. A few of the more enterprising ones we encountered came up with some clever ways to grab our attention.

Once, after an in-store appearance on our first tour, we came out to find that three girls had handcuffed themselves to the back of the motor home! Now, I've heard of girls following a band around, but this was a bit extreme. Making it more interesting was the fact that they didn't have the keys to the handcuffs. They seemed pretty intent on making sure they went with us to the next venue, but our tour manager wouldn't allow it. He picked the locks and off they went, like undersized fish thrown back in the water. We fired our tour manager the next day. No, just kidding!

Another time, I had checked into a hotel after an all-night drive. I was exhausted and just wanted to get a few hours' sleep. As soon as my head hit the pillow, the phone rang. It was a "maid."

"Excuse me, Mr. Ferrari, it's housekeeping. Just wanted to see if you needed the room made up."

"Uh, no thanks, we just checked in and the room's fine." I hung up the phone and started back to my much-needed beauty rest.

A minute later, the phone rang again. This time, it was a different voice. I noticed she was giggling a little. "Mr. Ferrari, hi, it's housekeeping. Just wanted to make sure you had enough soap and towels for your shower."

"Look, I'm fine, the room's fine, I don't need anything, and if you don't mind, I'm going to sleep for a few hours." All of a sudden I heard the other voice in the background, and now they're both giggling.

"Well, if you need any help with your shower, just call Kelly and Susan in housekeeping, OK?" Talk about room service!

MARC'S TIPS FOR THE ROAD

Along the way, I've learned a few things about being on the road. Here are a few tips and tricks that will hopefully make your time on the road a little easier and more rewarding.

Always Carry a Little Money and Change with You

On the road, plans change quickly and things happen spontaneously. You may decide to go for a ride with the three girls who show up at your hotel in a Mustang convertible, or accompany the local record company rep on his rounds to a few stores. If you get stuck without cash or identification (in case you happen to meet some of the local law enforcement), this can put you in a very awkward position. I mean, what happens if the girls turn out to be psychos bent on mutilating you? Say you ditch 'em somehow—now what? Or you happen to find a pawnshop that happens to have that rare guitar you've been looking for? *Always* carry money. Make sure you have some spare change for that all-important phone call you may need to make.

Always Know Where You're Staying

Grab a business card from the hotel, or write the address and phone number down on a piece of paper. Knowing that you're at the Motel 6 might not be enough info, as large cities may have several locations of the same chain. If you're visiting a city for the first time and aren't familiar with your surroundings, try to make a mental note of other businesses that are adjacent to the hotel. This may save you a lot of headaches later, especially if you've been partying and your memory is a little foggy. I know: It happened to me many a time on our first few tours. Having emergency numbers like those for the local promoter, the production telephone number, or your road manager's cellular number couldn't hurt, either.

Know Who You're Surrounding Yourself With

Most of the people you'll come into contact with on the road are strangers. You're just meeting these people for the first time, and you have no clue what they're really about. Granted, one of the most exciting things about being on the road *is* meeting new people, but nonetheless it pays to be cautious. Everyone has an agenda. Most are well-meaning; however, there are some vindictive types of people out there. A girl you met earlier in the day may have an overjealous boyfriend (or father) with a violent streak, who wants to teach a lesson to the pretty-boy rock star who comes gallivanting into town for just one night. Now, I'm not saying you should cloister yourself in your bus or hotel like a monk, but just be aware of the people you hang out with. Trust your gut instincts and intuitions—they're usually right.

Eat Healthy

It's bad enough that you don't sleep with any regularity on tour (which has the effect of causing *irregularity*). The least you can do is help your body adjust by eating properly. Truck-stop food isn't famous for being high on the health list, but at least you can avoid the fried, fatty foods on the menu. For breakfast, try ordering oatmeal instead of the typical artery-clogging bacon and eggs or such. Your heart and colon will love you for it. Try to stop at a supermarket from time to time to stock up on fresh food, whether it's veggies, fruit, healthy snacks, or microwavable, low-fat TV dinners. Most tour buses have a refrigerator of some sort. If you're in a van, you can buy a Styrofoam cooler. I know

LAY OFF THE MAYONNAISE!

On the subject of food, there is one major piece of advice I'd like to offer. It may even save your life. *Never, never, ever, under any circumstance whatsoever, eat anything with mayonnaise that's been sitting at the venue!* As a matter of fact, you'll be doing yourself a favor by not eating anything with mayonnaise *anytime* on tour, even from a so-called fancy restaurant. You're better off going a little hungry until you find something else than risking food poisoning. Mayonnaise is one of the most common culprits, as it spoils easily. Foods to keep away from include egg salad, tuna salad, potato salad, the whole works. Seafood is the other food that puts up a red flag. Unless you're familiar with where that fish has been, I'd stay away from it. Eating seafood salad is like playing Russian roulette. You may get away with it for a while, but eventually, it's gonna get you.

it's sometimes difficult to get to a health store or a regular supermarket, especially if you have to convince a whole busload of people to do it. But it's worth it in the long run.

Promoters are normally required to provide the band with a *rider*, which is a list of items the band requests, such as certain food items, drinks, supplies, and so on. The promoter is normally required to provide meals for the band and crew, either in the form of cash (to go out and get your own meal), a catered dinner, or the most common, the infamous *deli tray*. Deli trays normally consist of cold cuts, veggies, fruit, and the various mayonnaise-based salads noted above. The problem with deli trays is that you never know how fresh they are. They could've been prepared three days ago, for all you know. They could've been sitting in a hot van or truck several hours before being delivered. Half the time, they've been sitting in the venue uncovered for who knows how long. The flies have found it well before you have, trust me. What happens if someone around is sick? This is a communal meal, let's not forget. You get the point. It's bad enough that deli meat in general is unhealthy. That's why I used to bring my own food whenever possible. I realize that this is not always practical or even possible, but just realize that you're taking a risk of some sort any time you eat food without knowing how it was prepared.

Getting back to the rider: This is your opportunity to request some of the types of things you may otherwise have to make a special trip to the store for, so at least try to ask for some healthy-type foods. If the promoter provides you with a six-pack of your favorite Ginseng soda, or a package of veggie burgers, snag it and put it in your bag for later. I used to keep a few gallon-sized Ziploc bags around to keep things that I wanted. You may have a travel day next and not be able to get to the store, so it's good to stock up whenever possible.

I've heard about riders for some bigger headline bands that had some pretty ridiculous requests, such as gourmet caviar, French champagne, Cuban cigars, exotic dishes, and hard-to-find candies. I've also heard of riders that requested a lot of nonfood items such as boxes of condoms, strippers, power tools, and so on. A famous story about riders involves Van Halen. Supposedly, their rider requested, among other things, M&M candies, but the stipulation was that there were to be no brown ones. Their point was they wanted the promoters to take their rider seriously, as it was part of their contract!

Save Money on Your Phone Bill

Make your phone calls from the production phone. Using the phones at your hotel is a sure bet to run up a huge phone bill. Many hotels tack a surcharge onto long distance calls, and most times you're getting billed at the highest rate, anyway. Phone cards are not that much better. Take advantage of the production phone at the gig (or if in a club, use the phone in the club's office) to make your calls. You may not be able to gab to your heartbroken lonely girlfriend back home for hours on end, but at least you'll be able to get a few calls in and save some of your hard-earned money. I learned an expensive lesson in Japan when I got an $80 phone bill on a five-minute call. You can also work out a "call-back" arrangement with someone if he or she has your itinerary. Ring once or twice, hang up, and let him or her call *you* back. Or, you can call person-to-person collect for yourself; the other party will refuse the charge and know it's time to call you back. Sometimes, the operator will let you leave a number doing it this way. The advent of cell phones with generous packages has made calling a lot more convenient, but you still have to foot the bill, so talk on someone else's dime whenever possible.

Be Prepared

Don't get caught running out of "must-have" things with months to go on a tour. Take your favorite things with you. If you have a special shampoo that you use, a particular vitamin or protein shake you like, a favorite local beer you gotta have, whatever it is, be sure you take enough of it with you to last the whole tour. Don't assume that you'll be able to find it in some small, out-of-the-way town in North Dakota—or even in other

major cities, for that matter. Regardless of the availability of
your necessities, there usually isn't enough time or the means to
go on a wild goose chase to find this special item.

Think "Safety"

If you're traveling overseas, take a photocopy of your passport
and driver's license. Make sure to keep these separate from your
originals. If your original passport *is* lost, you're still gonna be in
a whole heap of trouble, but at least you'll have some temporary
identification that may be honored in certain circumstances. It's
not a bad idea to keep the phone numbers of the local hospitals
and embassies in your wallet. If you get arrested in a foreign
country, remember that you are bound by *their* laws. (Remember
Midnight Express?) The embassy may not be able to extricate
you from your predicament, but it should always be your first
call in times of serious trouble.

Remember Your Friends

The simple act of sending someone a note or a postcard may
not seem like a big deal to you, but trust me, it means a hell of a
lot on the other end. The minute or two you spend jotting
down a few words can help make an everlasting impression on
someone. I used to make it a point at least once a year to mail a
postcard to all the reps and their secretaries at the label, all our
endorsers, all our business contacts, as many people in the fan
club as humanly possible. And, of course, all my relatives. (At
least those I still wanted to have some contact with!) It's sur-
prising how few musicians remember these people—a postcard
will go a long way in the "good will" department. It makes
everyone feel important that you would take some time out of
your hectic schedule to remember them. It's an investment of so
little time and money that will pay off in droves. Besides, what
else better is there to do on one of those ten-hour drives?

Keep a Diary or Scrapbook

Being on tour is one of the most exciting things you'll ever do.
It is truly a life experience that you may never repeat. As you

may be bombarded by a barrage of never-ending events that leave you little or no free time, it's a good idea to try to capture your adventure for future posterity. Take pictures—lots of them. Buy a video camera, if you can, and make your own road documentary of your travels. Keep a souvenir from each city, such as a postcard, a brochure, a ticket stub, or a restaurant matchbook. You'll be surprised at how many memories these will bring back months or years after the fact.

Enjoy Life

Borrowing another phrase from *Spinal Tap:* "Have a good time all the time."

On stage with Ron Keel and Jack Daniels.
© 1986 Joe Giron.

In-store appearances are one of the best ways to bring artists together with their fans, and they are a very effective marketing tool. This photo is from an in-store appearance supporting our fourth album, called *Keel*.
Photo credit: Marc Ferrari.

Life's a party.
Photo credit: Jodi Summers.

CHAPTER 7
The Big Picture: Wake-Up Calls, Solo Careers, and Reality Checks

All good things must come to an end. It's a fact of life we all have to accept. Whether it's a great vacation, a business venture, a marriage, or even a fairy tale, there comes a time when we must wake up from the dream and accept the inevitable. Unfortunately, in the midst of something enjoyable or successful, most people don't want to believe that the good times will come to an end; therefore, long-range vision can become dangerously shortsighted. There is a tendency to think that the good times will last forever, or that things will only get better. It is the wise person who can foresee impending changes and has a contingency plan ready to be implemented at short notice. Oftentimes, this can mean the difference between future success or failure.

A career in the music industry is like a carnival ride: lots of turbulent motion, lights, sounds, action, thrills, chills, excitement, and uncertainty. Some get to ride several times, others just once. Most people enjoy the ride, but there are those who find out they don't like it once they're on. Some people decide to get off the ride, sometimes temporarily, other times permanently. Those who get off may find there's a long line to get back on, and, sometimes, they never get that second ride. Some get off voluntarily, but others have the ride abruptly stopped by unforeseen circumstances. No one wants to get stuck at the top of the Ferris wheel. It's a frustrating, scary feeling. But it does occur. I should know: It happened to me.

GETTING DROPPED FROM YOUR RECORD CONTRACT

Most record contracts contain a clause that allows the record company the opportunity to continue its relationship with you. This is done on an album-by-album basis, known as an *option*. If someone says he has a seven-album deal with a label, it actually means that the label has the *right* to release up to seven albums of material from the artist. It doesn't guarantee that the label will call for all seven albums and release them. As discussed earlier, it may not guarantee that the label will even release the *first* one. If the label is not contractually obligated, it indeed has the right to record the album and not release it! If you are a successful artist and are selling lots of records, it is reasonable to assume that the record company will want to exercise the option to continue putting out your records. After all, you are making the company some money. However, if you are deemed to be a financial drain on the label, it may decide not to continue the relationship and cut its losses. A label may keep releasing an artist's product while the artist is hot, but as soon as sales falter, it may let the artist go from the contract. This option is normally at the record company's sole discretion, since only the biggest artists are in a position to demand the exclusion of this option in their contracts. Some artists are able to negotiate a time frame in which this option is to be exercised, such as after a tour has been completed, or after a certain video is released. However, this is not always the case, and a label can release a band from its contract at the most inopportune times.

In June 1990 my second band, Cold Sweat, released our debut album, titled *Break Out*, on MCA Records. Produced by Kevin Beamish (REO Speedwagon, Jefferson Starship, Y&T, Saxon), it was warmly received by the press, who showered it with overwhelmingly positive reviews. We toured the whole summer in support of the album, opening for national acts such as Dio, Sleeze Beez, and Savatage. In September of that year, we were invited to Europe to open up for Whitesnake and Aerosmith at the prestigious *Monsters of Rock* festival, which drew over 50,000 people! We were continually building our fan base and enjoying significant sales in the markets in which we appeared. In addition, we were beginning to get critical radio airplay and MTV acceptance, and it seemed that the momentum the band had generated would allow us to break away from the pack and go on to commercial success. In October of that year, we began our first headline tour, playing midsized clubs on the East Coast. The band was in great spirits, the label was happy with our progress, and everything seemed like it was finally falling into place.

Three weeks later, after a particularly good show in Washington, D.C., I got a call from our manager at the club. Immediately, from the tone of her voice, I could tell that something was wrong. I braced myself for the worst. "Marc, MCA Records has decided not to pick up the option for another record." I went silent for almost a minute, almost in shock, trying to absorb the news and make some sense out of it. A million and one thoughts raced through my head—how could the label do this to us, after all the time and effort that went into making this record and supporting it?

The album had been out for only five months, hardly a fair amount of time to judge an album, never mind an entire career. MCA had spent almost $250,000 on the recording, mixing, album artwork, video, tour support, and promotional items. The band had even spent some of its *own* money on independent press and promotion, which we did as an act of faith in our label and ourselves. We were given no indication whatsoever that there was any cause for alarm; it hit us like a sucker punch from out of the blue. I felt like someone had pushed me out of a moving car in the middle of the desert after riding with the driver for thousands of miles.

When I asked for a reason for this abrupt "divorce," my manager said that the label told her that it was restructuring and that several people who were key supporters of our band were going to be let go. In essence, we were *orphaned*, which, unfortunately, happens quite frequently in the music business.

Orphaned is a term used when a band loses key people at the label who are proponents or benefactors. They may include the A&R rep who signed the band (as in our case), or people in the promotional or marketing departments who were really pushing for the band. When new people come to a label (especially in the A&R department), they very often will make a clean sweep of the roster, wanting to start fresh with artists that *they* signed, not their predecessors.

You would think that a company would want to protect an investment of over a quarter-million dollars. You would think that a company would have the decency to allow creative artists the fair chance to prove themselves; after all, the label went to the effort to sign the band in the first place. You would think that a company would have the foresight to know that success is not always an immediate return, but a steady climb. Careers are made over the long haul, not the short race. Dropping a band this early in its career has no real logic to it whatsoever. However, this is the record business, and things that most people think are logical or practical don't always apply. As a matter of fact, they *very rarely* apply.

We wound up finishing the dates we had scheduled, then returned home to Los Angeles to regroup and figure out our next move. Needless to say, it was a long, somber trip back home—the reality check to end all reality checks.

Getting released from a label is often (but not always) a fatal blow to an artist. It demoralizes the artist, disrupts momentum, and has the tendency to brand the artist as "tainted goods." Labels may view a dropped band as problematic, or worse yet, incapable of success, when, in fact, it was the label that was problematic. This is perhaps the most unfair outgrowth, since in the majority of cases, it wasn't the artist's fault at all that this occurred. Many times, bands feel so frustrated, discouraged, or disheartened that they break up. Indeed, it takes a lot of courage and inner strength to pick oneself up from a setback of such magnitude, but the strong ones always do, and that's why they're survivors. It's like a boxer who gets knocked down to the canvas but finds it within himself to get back up and win the fight. Being down doesn't have to mean being out, and although you may not see the positive in a negative situation, everything in life happens for a good reason. It's been said that what doesn't kill you only makes you stronger. Use a situation such as this one to fortify yourself for future endeavors, and you will be the wiser and better for it.

SOLO CAREERS

Having the rug pulled out from under you is bad enough because, for the most part, it's beyond your control. However, some artists commit virtual career suicide (careericide?) by messing with a good thing when they have it. The most common form of "careericide" is the *solo career*. Even those in the most successful bands sometimes do not see the forest for the trees. Human nature, combined with the volatility of working in a band environment, almost inevitably leads to thoughts of solo career fancy. All of a sudden, individuals in a band feel they can do better on their own. They may feel that it is primarily because of *them* that their band is so successful and therefore they are entitled to a bigger portion of the spotlight or financial rewards. Perhaps they feel creatively stifled and are not able to fully express themselves in the confines of the give-and-take relationship of a band.

However, it has been proven time and time again (especially in the genre of rock) that audiences identify with the *group of individuals* and not with the *individuals of the group*. The sum of the parts is invariably greater than the parts alone. A possible exception would be the Beatles, who were a phenomenon unto themselves. Each of the Beatles had fans that were loyal to their favorite members, although it should be mentioned that these fans were loyal to the whole group as well as their favorite individual. By the way, George Harrison and John Lennon released solo albums while they were in the Beatles, but neither one generated sales anywhere near the band's sales. Most people don't even know the names of those albums!

Other times, solo albums are done strictly as a "breather" from the band, with the intention of returning to the band fold once the album is finished. A good example of this would be the solo albums from each of the four members of KISS, which came out in 1978. In a rather unique situation, they were released at the same time, with coordinating artwork and marketing campaigns, and with the full understanding that the four would continue on as KISS afterwards. That way, each of them had the opportunity to explore some avenues that they may not have been able to in KISS. In this way, blowing off some musical steam can be very healthy and prevent unnecessary frustrations from arising. It may have prevented the band from breaking up prematurely, prolonging their lucrative career as a unit. Each member of the Rolling Stones has done solo albums throughout the years, but they always reunite for the group recordings. Same with Genesis, although Phil Collins is in the enviable position of having had both a successful band career *and* a solo career at the same time.

When band members decide to leave a band permanently and strike out on their own, they are rolling the dice with their career. It is very rare that a member leaves a successful band and then goes on to an equally or more successful career. Sure, there are examples like Peter Frampton (Humble Pie), Peter Gabriel (Genesis), Ozzy Osbourne (Black Sabbath), Lionel Richie (The Commodores), Steve Winwood (Traffic), Robin Trower (Procol Harum), and Gary Moore (Thin Lizzy). But, again, these are the exceptions and not the rule. Being a member of one of the world's biggest bands still doesn't guarantee any level of long-term solo success. There are hundreds upon hundreds of solo albums by members of hugely popular bands, but surprisingly few of these have gone on to any measurable success. Case in point: Solo albums by members of such luminous bands as Aerosmith, Guns n' Roses, Pearl Jam, Soundgarden, Rush, Journey, or even the Rolling Stones have largely gone unnoticed.

If you're going to jump ship, you'd better make damn sure you have another ship to jump *to,* and that the second ship is as seaworthy as the first! If you are leaving a business partnership as well, you may be forfeiting monies that are due you. Can you afford to do this? Fans can be very fickle, and that safety net you thought you had may not be there when you take that leap. I'm reminded of a song by Cinderella, based on an old saying— "You Don't Know What You've Got Until It's Gone." Take a long, hard look at the big picture before you decide to do something radical like leaving your band. Ask yourself a few questions: Do I really have the ability to do this alone? Am I secure enough in my career to risk the loss of momentum by starting over? Will this action resolve the issues that are leading to this decision, or just create new ones?

LEAVING MEMBER CLAUSES

Some artists who believe they are in a bad record contract think that they can wipe the slate clean by leaving a band, thus starting over fresh. What a lot of artists don't realize is that in most cases, the label has a *leaving member clause* in their contract that each member is bound to. This allows the label to have the first option to retain the recording services of the artist as a solo entity, which is why most albums from solo artists are on the same label as the band they were in. (By the way, leaving member clauses are another major negotiating point for that brilliant lawyer you hopefully retained.)

Say you happened to become a star in your own right within the framework of the band. The label may think you have the potential to be a commercial success and exercise this option. The label's standpoint is that it has nurtured the artist's career up to this point and has invested a considerable amount of time, effort, and money in that career. Therefore, it is only protecting its investment by retaining your recording services.

Conversely, the label may feel that you would not be a commercially viable solo entity and will therefore decline its option. This option is normally made within thirty to ninety days after you give written notification to the label that you are leaving the group, depending on your contract. If the label decides not to exercise this option, you are then free to negotiate with other labels. If the label keeps you, however, you will generally be bound to the *same terms* (if not worse) as your original contract. These major points generally include the advance, point structure, accounting terms, and duration of term.

So, if you're trying to get out of your recording contract, simply leaving a band is not the surefire way out. It may even make a bad situation worse. If you decide to leave or go solo, you may be in for a few bumps. The next chapter will provide some ideas on how to stay financially solvent during some tough times.

CHAPTER 8
The Money Game: Keeping in Green When Times Get Lean

I have a theory about success in the music industry. I liken it to playing a slot machine. If you stay at it long enough, it will pay off. For some people, the payoff comes a little more quickly than for others. Some invest a little, others a fortune. The trick is harnessing that payoff and hopefully investing it in other means or areas to sustain yourself.

FOLLOWING THE DOLLAR

One of the biggest misconceptions most people have about the music industry is just how much money everyone makes. Sure, the top-draw bands can make millions, but they are a small percentage of the masses who play live and put out albums. Compared to the total number of musicians who actually play recreationally, semiprofessionally, or professionally, the "millionaire" musician is literally one in a million. A lot of up-and-coming musicians think that if they get signed to a major-label record deal, they'll be on easy street, their problems over. Actually, their problems are only beginning. It's tough enough just to get signed. Only a fraction of the people who try actually do it. Bear in mind the odds just to clear this hurdle. And even if you do get signed (and you *can* do it!), there are no guarantees. It's not like a sports star who at least gets a salary whether he plays or not, or whether he's injured or not. In music, a good part of your income is based on royalties, and there's no predicting just how much these royalties, if any, will be.

Clearing that first hurdle and getting a major-label record contract is a monumental feat. Your second hurdle is becoming successful once you've been signed. The statistics show that only five out of every one hundred major-label releases in the United States goes *gold* (500,000 units sold), a benchmark that is generally recognized as the normal "break-even" point on a typical record. That, of course, all depends on the structure of your deal, the amount you took as an advance, and various other recoupable charges such as the cost of making the record and the expenses of tour support, video costs, promotional monies spent, and so on. But, generally speaking, 500,000 units is a ballpark figure on when you could expect to be recouped to your record company and back to a zero-level balance. However, there are nineteen-to-one odds that you won't hit that mark, given those statistics.

Hey, I'm not here to preach doom and gloom, nor am I trying to dissuade you from following your dreams. You shouldn't be pursuing a career in rock 'n' roll solely for financial gain anyway—it should be for the love of the music first. What I am trying to do is point out that the money can be like a mirage—you may think you see it, but it's not really there. If you're going to climb all the way to the top of the mountain, just don't be disappointed by the view from the top: It may not be exactly what you think it *should* be.

It's no secret that musicians (and other members of the creative community) normally have to struggle to get recognized. Most musicians struggle all through their careers. Achieving a level of moderate success does not guarantee that one will have enough money to live an entire life on. As a matter of fact, even those bands in the top fifth percentile that do make decent money don't make enough to sustain themselves for more than a few years.

I read a statistic about baseball players. The average salary in the major leagues is nearly $2 million per year. However, the average career span of a major league baseball player is just five years. After a player's baseball career is over, he has to find other means to support himself. And even though major league baseball has a pension plan, it's quite possible that he will have to come up with additional income in order to survive.

Individuals in ultrasuccessful bands can gross the same amount of money in the same time period as a baseball player, for sure. Interestingly enough, the average career of a signed, major-label act is a scant three years. For every band like the Rolling Stones, Z.Z. Top, or Aerosmith that have been around twenty-five years or more, there are hundreds of bands that do one or two albums and then are dropped, or break up. Now, a million dollars may seem like a lot, but after agent commissions, business management commissions, and, of course, taxes (which may be up to 40 percent), there may not be a whole lot left to that pot of gold. Go through a drug problem or a divorce, and you could be in the red sooner than you know it. Therefore, it is imperative to have not only a financial plan in mind to put your hard-earned money to work for you (which is one of the functions of your business manager), but also a game plan to diversify your earning potential, so that you're not entirely reliant on your record royalties. There's an old saying: "Catch a man a fish and he eats for a day. Teach a man to fish and he eats for life."

Most bands earn their greatest income on the road. When you're touring, you're hopefully generating record sales, which, in turn, generate record royalties and publishing income. Although these monies take months to filter back down to you, it's all "money in the bank." Of course, your merchandising profits will be the most immediate return. If you've recouped against your merchandising advance, you may even get a weekly draw from the company. When a band comes off the road, there may be some time before the next advance kicks in or before the next royalty statement is due. Often, bands have to scrape by while these additional monies are forthcoming, and this can make for some lean times.

TEN WAYS TO SUPPLEMENT YOUR INCOME

There are a number of different ways a musician can supplement his income without sacrificing his integrity. No one *wants* to get a menial job at a fast-food place or warehouse, but if push comes to shove, it has to be done. Hey, Ozzy Osbourne worked in a slaughterhouse for awhile! Musicians have God-given talents, and it's always better when these talents can be used in music-related situations. Below are but a few ways to keep in the green when the going gets lean.

1. Teaching

By nature most musicians are outgoing, gregarious, interactive, and people-friendly. Teaching is a natural extension of this and is a perfect choice as a means to provide a good income. Having your instrument in your hands is an added bonus, too—it'll keep your playing and reading chops up. I started teaching when I was thirteen and continued until I moved to California. At one point I had thirty students per week! During my touring days, I had several students who were very understanding and would come over when I was in town for a break. I continue to teach a handful of students to this day, although I think I learn more from them (about current music styles) than they learn from me! Typical hourly rates for guitar lessons range from $15–$50, depending on the teacher or location. If you're working out of a music store, the store may take a cut. Joe Satriani, who is currently one of the most successful instrumental rock guitarists around, is one musician who started out as a teacher. Not only did he get a record deal, but several of his students did, too, such as Steve Vai (Frank Zappa, David Lee Roth, Whitesnake, and solo), Kirk Hammett (Metallica), Larry LaLonde (Possessed, Primus), and Danny Gill (Hericane Alice, Speak No Evil)!

2. Studio Work

Doing session work can be very lucrative. Scale pay for a Musicians' Union-sanctioned session starts at $250 for the first eight hours in certain locales. You'll also get "reuse fees" if these recordings wind up in other ancillary uses such as movies, TV shows, or re-released albums. Top-notch musicians can command double- or even triple-scale payment. Your local chapter of the Musicians' Union can help you get into this field and may even have a referral service. Steve Lukather of Toto is the prime example of someone who has a successful career as both a studio musician and a recording artist. Before Toto went on to sell millions of albums, Steve had established himself as one of Los Angeles's most in-demand players, a position he still holds today. If you are a featured performer on someone else's album, you may need to get permission from your record company, because normally you are signed exclusively to your label for your recording services.

Vocalists can earn even more in the extremely lucrative commercial market. A national commercial campaign can earn tens of thousands of dollars in residual royalties for the vocalist, in addition to his production fees for the session. The top guys can make more than a million dollars per year! Michael Bolton was one of the most sought-after singers in the jingle business before he rose to fame as a solo artist. His voice could be heard in commercials for many national companies, including Budweiser and Burger King.

3. Producing

If the studio is your bag, then you may want to consider producing. Having a background in audio engineering is certainly a plus, but not entirely necessary. There are some major producers who do not know how to engineer sessions, but they offer valuable insights in song construction, arrangements, and guidance. Some have their own "style" or "sound" that is recognizable, and others are known for being motivators and for bringing out the best performances from artists. As discussed in chapter 4, producers get paid a set fee or *points* on the album, or both, and they can make millions of dollars from a successful album. While you may not be able to command these kinds of terms now, you can certainly start by working with up-and-coming bands that may be close to getting signed. If you happen to produce the demos that get the band signed, the label or band may ask you to do the album. It worked for Glen Ballard—he started writing with Alanis Morissette very early on, and the demos he produced actually became the finished album. That album has gone on to become the greatest-selling debut album ever, selling over 15 million copies in the United States alone. Glen has gone on to become one of the most sought-after producers in the industry.

4. Touring with Other Artists or Productions

Going out as a salaried member of another band (or production) may be just the ticket to earning money as a true "playing" musician. There's nothing like playing every night to keep your chops up to par. Just be sure your own band won't need you around first! If you're about to start writing or rehearsing for your next album, you may not be able to leave for several months. However, if you're not involved in the writing process, and you're itching to hit the road, this may be just the right thing. Some of the bigger gigs with established artists or productions (such as cruise ships, Ice Capades, and circuses) may be union-sanctioned, so you may have to be a union member first to get one of these gigs. Your salary will depend on a lot of different factors, such as the status of the artist (and yours), the length of the tour, and ancillary buyouts for home videos, talk shows, award shows, live albums, and so on. Top guys can get up to $10,000 per week, but the normal range is $1,500–$5,000 plus *per diems*, a daily allowance for food or other incidentals. Of course, if you're filling in for your best friend's grunge rock band on a club tour of North Dakota, the figures may be a decimal point less!

5. Pickup and Side Bands

Bored with your main band but don't want to play second fiddle to someone else? Start a second "side" or pickup band. Lots of major label artists have had success with side bands. As a matter of fact, many of them get signed to deals as well! Usually, they will be on the same label as their original band, as the label has an option built in for solo deals. Or, perhaps, it's just for fun and a little "beer money" at local gigs. Either way, a side band can be a rewarding break from the usual grind, bringing some fun and spontaneity while stimulating some new creative energy.

6. Sidelining

Sidelining involves playing "on camera" on TV shows or movies. Most times, the musicians are not actually playing live, but rather "playing" to a prerecorded song. Sidelining work is usually filtered through the Musicians' Union; therefore, you must be a member in good standing to get referred. There is a minimum rate of about $225 for the first ten hours, depending on locale. Not exactly a huge amount of money, but it beats digging a ditch. You may earn additional royalties through *reuse fees* (similar to those you may earn doing studio work), which occur when the movie or TV show is sold into secondary markets that were not included in the first use of your performance. Most of the time, you're just standing around waiting for the scene to be set up; it's actually pretty boring. If you're tempted to get involved just for the glamour aspect, you're in for a big disappointment.

My first sidelining gig came about very coincidentally. When I was in Keel, we had a song on the soundtrack for a movie called *Dudes,* which starred Jon Cryer and was directed by Penelope Spheeris. Penelope was very much into music, and I always used to see her out in the clubs around Los Angeles—we'd have a drink and catch up. When I read about her being hired for *Wayne's World,* I gave her a call, thinking I might be able to get some of my songs in the movie. I sent her a few tapes and didn't hear anything back for the longest time. One day, I came home to an answering machine message from the casting director. Seems that Penelope had found my tape under a pile of papers, and it reminded her to call me for a gig—she needed a sideline guitarist! Talk about being at the right place at the right time!

Working on that film was one of the most amazing experiences of my life. Even though the hours were pretty long (normally sixteen hours a day), it was a pleasure being around both the cast and the crew. We always had a riot. Mike Myers and Dana Carvey always kept us in stitches, and Tia Carrere was equally great to work with. I wound up working about two weeks on the set. The movie went on to become one of the biggest smash hits of the year, taking a lot of people by surprise. Two years later, when they made the sequel, we were asked back. Our role was not quite as prominent for the sequel, but it was still a great time. I got to do a scene with Christopher Walken (one of my favorite actors), and another one with Aerosmith. Peter Frampton was also supposed to be in *Wayne's World II*—he had a scene at the *Waynestock* concert, but it was cut out. I remember hanging out with him in his trailer for awhile—a thrill for me, as he was one of my biggest influences.

Because those movies achieved a certain degree of success, I started to get requests to do other sideline work and went on to do the TV shows *Murder, She Wrote* and *Step by Step*.

From the set of *Wayne's World;* left to right, George Foster, Anthony Focx, Rob Lowe, and the author.
Photo credit: Marc Ferrari.

From the set of *Wayne's World 2*; left to right, me, Tia Carrere, and Steven Tyler.
Photo credit: Elliot Marks, courtesy Paramount Pictures.

7. Film and TV Scoring

Writing music for film or TV projects can be one of the most lucrative areas for a musician to break into. The top film composers can command up to several hundred thousand dollars for a score to a big film. The residual income from public performances (ASCAP, BMI, or SESAC) can multiply this severalfold. Composers who write the weekly music for a TV show are normally hired by the studio or the production company and are paid a weekly salary, which can range from $5,000 on up. Of course, performance income will increase this figure dramatically. Just to give you a general idea of the kind of money you can earn when a song is on TV, consider this: A *full feature performance* on a network TV show during prime time (7:00 P.M.–11:00 P.M.) can generate upwards of $1,500 per use under the right circumstances. The performance rights organizations have different criteria and weighing formulas for feature performances, but they are comparable under similar circumstances. With ASCAP, a full feature performance has to have a vocal and last forty-five seconds or longer in duration.

If you had five or six full feature performances per week as a composer, the income would be astronomical! Also, if the show happens to repeat at a later date, your public performance society will pay you again for it. You'll also earn residuals from foreign territories if these shows happen to air there as well.

The best example of a performing artist who made the switch to film composition is Danny Elfman, formerly of Oingo Boingo. Even though Oingo Boingo was a moderately successful band, Danny has really made his mark in the film field, where he has quickly become one of the most sought-after and highly paid composers. Movies featuring his scores include *Edward Scissorhands, Nightmare Before Christmas,* several of the Batman movies, *Extreme Measures, Men in Black, Planet of the Apes,* and many others. Other famous rockers who have tried their hand at film composition include Eric Clapton (*Rush*), Tom Petty (*She's the One*), and Neil Young (*Dead Man*). It may be a little difficult to convince a major picture production to use a first-time composer, so you may have to work your way up, just as you must with anything else. To gain experience in the field, you may want to intern for a working composer or perhaps approach an up-and-coming filmmaker and offer your services at a reduced rate (or for free, just to get your foot in the door the first time). Who knows? That up-and-coming filmmaker may just turn out to be the next Steven Spielberg. All of a sudden, you become the most in-demand composer by association.

One of the great things about composing for film or TV is that you can do this as long as you can play. Going on the road and jumping around the stage may get a little taxing for those who are past their physical prime. You don't have to look like Adonis, run around like a possessed rooster, or wear chains and leather to have a successful career in this field. You could, however, balance things out to accommodate both your band career and your film career if you wanted. All the above-mentioned artists have.

8. Opening a Studio

Those musicians who are technically adept may consider opening their own studio. Wherever there are musicians, there is going to be the need for recording facilities, and who better to know and understand the needs of a musician than another musician? Besides, you could use the studio for your own projects as well. By the way, here is a smart idea that some bands have done and you should consider: Instead of taking your record company advance and recording at someone else's studio, why not buy your own recording equipment and make the album yourselves? After the record is done, you'll have the gear for future projects—perhaps even opening your studio for rental, which can provide an income for you forever. You'll have to convince your record company that you have the ability to record yourself professionally, but this has been done on several occasions that I know of. Major-label recording budgets can range from $50,000 to $500,000—that's a lot of recording gear you could purchase for that same money. Studio equipment keeps getting better while prices keep decreasing, so it's a great opportunity to make an investment in your future, which can pay off in hefty dividends.

Lots of musicians have opened studios, but three of the most famous include ABBA (Polar Studios in Stockholm), the Rolling Stones (Rolling Stones Mobile Studio), and Heart (Bad Animals Studio in Seattle), all of which have become world-renowned facilities. Having your own studio will also force you to become better at engineering, providing opportunities to segue over to producing bands as well.

9. Music Store or Equipment Representative

Taking a job at a music store can be the perfect "in-between" job—it keeps you surrounded by music and musicians and can offer fringe benefits, such as equipment discounts and flexible hours. While most musicians don't like to have to work a "day job" if they don't have to, at least this is a hands-on, industry-related gig, not a degrading, menial-labor job.

Becoming a representative for an equipment manufacturer is another avenue to consider. You would conceivably be servicing music stores or other accounts in your geographic area, earning a set salary, commission, or combination of both. Full-time field reps for major musical industry product lines can earn six-figure annual incomes. Of course, if you're touring you can't do this full-time, but you may be able to make some decent supplemental income on a part-time basis, and you could keep your contact base for the future, should you decide to do it permanently.

10. Starting a Label or Publishing Company

You've heard the old saying, "If you can't beat 'em, join 'em." Nowhere does this apply more aptly than in the music business. Many musicians who have grown increasingly frustrated with the major-label game have taken matters into their own hands and formed their own independent companies. They have become the masters of their own destinies and in some cases have made millions doing it. The independent spirit has always been a driving force in industry, be it musical or otherwise. In the entertainment sector, independents have a genuine chance to stand up to the majors and carve out a decent market share. (Miramax Films is the prime example in the film industry. They started from humble beginnings and grew into one of the most powerful forces around, developing several Academy Award–winning films.) The music industry has its share of success stories as well. The most famous example is Apple Records, started by the Beatles in 1968. The Beatles also created a whole self-contained organization that signed other artists (James Taylor, Badfinger, Mary Hopkins, Jackie Lomax, and others) and branched off into film production and other ventures. Unfortunately, primarily because of mismanagement, Apple folded, but not before the Beatles had created the standard by which all others have since been judged. Soon after, other major artists wanted their own labels. The Rolling Stones had theirs (Rolling Stones Records), as did Elton John (Rocket Records) and Led Zeppelin, whose Swan Song label had considerable success, primarily with Bad Company. Some of these labels were just vanity affairs, funded by the group's parent label; they really didn't function as a label in the true sense, but rather served as a toy to appease some superstar egos.

More recently, there have been a few success stories worth mentioning. Perhaps the biggest would be Epitaph Records, formed by ex–Bad Religion member Brett Gurewitz. Starting out on a shoestring, he began by releasing material from bands that were personal favorites, who he felt deserved better treatment than they were getting by the majors. His business started in his garage but grew quickly. In 1993 he signed a band from Southern California called Offspring. One thing led to another, and Offspring caught on like wildfire. The band went on to sell over 6 million copies of *Smash* in the United States alone, making it the greatest-selling independent release in history. Needless to say, Epitaph became a player in the field. The label has earned well-deserved respect by continuing to hold true to its independent roots. In spite of tremendous success, Epitaph has persistently resisted lucrative offers from major companies wanting to buy out the label.

Some other successes include American Recordings, started by impresario Rick Rubin, who signed the Black Crowes; Metal Blade, started by Brian Slagel, who helped to launch the heavy metal boom of the early 1980s showcasing bands such as Metallica and Ratt; and the Shrapnel label, started by my old buddy Mike Varney, himself a former musician.

On the publishing side, Bob-A-Lew Music, which was cofounded by Bonnie Raitt and Huey Lewis, has become a very prominent company, enjoying a lot of success with major hits and film and TV activity. Publishing also happens to be the route I've taken.

Many years ago, I began to realize that I had to diversify if I wanted to make a decent living in the music business. Although I had achieved a certain level of success with my past accomplishments, I was not being financially rewarded in proportion to that success. It's unfortunate that talent and financial success don't always go hand in hand, but those are the breaks. The cold reality I faced was that I needed to have an income stream that was going to be more consistent and constant than record royalties. I was always acutely aware of music publishing (the "gift that keeps on giving") and decided to focus my attention there. I wasn't exactly sure how I was going to get that foot in the door, but once I did, the rest of me was going to be sure to break that door down.

Los Angeles is undoubtedly the movie capital of the world. There is more entertainment content being produced in L.A. than anywhere else on the planet. I had been living in L.A. for nearly a decade, but being surrounded by the film and TV industry all this time, I hadn't seen the forest for the trees. I didn't give much thought to the opportunities for music in this sector. I had always been more concerned with making records and touring. Of course, like most other musicians and songwriters, I had a backlog of demos that I had been recording throughout the years. That's what songwriters do, right? But what to do with all these songs that weren't being used on the records I was making?

I had a friend who was working on a low-budget "B" movie. He was an assistant coffeemaker or something like that—not exactly high on the film industry food chain. Anyway, he was working on this film that had a few bar scenes in it. He overheard the director ask someone to find some rock music for these scenes, so he asked me if I would like to submit a few of my songs that were just "hanging around."

Well, wouldn't you know it; they loved the songs and wound up using two of them. They paid me $250 apiece and gave me a screen credit. I was astonished. I had earned a quick $500 for licensing something that already existed. Right there and then, the ol' lightbulb went off in my head. I hadn't given any thought to trying to place songs in film or TV, but obviously there was some need for it, as evidenced by what had just transpired. I figured if I could place a few songs in shows once in awhile, I would at the very least have some "beer money" to supplement my income. I decided to investigate this avenue further. I put together my best material and made up some sampler cassettes. I also had a logo designed and had stationery, business cards, envelopes, cassette labels, and J-cards done up. (Had to make it seem like I was a pro!) I then got hold of some industry sourcebooks and publications like the *Hollywood Reporter* and *Variety* and just started calling anyone and everyone! I introduced myself as an independent music publisher who had a wide range of master-quality recordings that I controlled and asked permission to send along these sampler tapes for possible music needs. I also stressed the fact that I was extremely flexible in licensing terms, as I controlled both the composition (the copyright) and the actual recording of it (the master). At the same time, I was expanding my catalog of songs that I was representing. I didn't want to be limited to just hard rock and heavy metal, so I put the word out to as many musicians as I knew. Soon, I had a wide variety of different styles of music, such as dance, R&B, country, blues, reggae, jazz, and techno.

Initially, I had success with some other "B" movie companies who couldn't afford the big dollars the major publishers were charging for their songs. By offering album-quality recordings at a fraction of the going rate, I was able to provide a cost-effective alternative for these companies. Although it took a while to get a break at some of the bigger companies, little by little, those breaks began to happen. One of my first breaks was with Disney. I made a "cold call" to someone in the music-publishing department who just happened to be looking for some rock music for a picture called *Life With Mikey*, starring Michael J. Fox. Due to impeccable timing, one of my songs was chosen: It was the first major film that had some of my music in it! Although the filmmakers used only fifteen or twenty seconds, I made some good money on it. Soon thereafter, other Disney films followed, including *Blank Check, Fatherhood, Mighty Ducks 2, Man of the House, A Kid in King Arthur's Court, Money for Nothing, Celtic Pride,* and *Ransom.*

I also caught a break at Paramount, where a little luck worked in my favor. I was reading the trade papers and happened to catch an article that mentioned that the head of the music department happened to be from Rochester, New York— very close to my hometown. I took this to be a good omen and used this as my introduction when I called him. Turns out I was right; Paramount has turned out to be one of my best clients. I have had songs in over fifty Paramount TV shows, including *Entertainment Tonight,* the *Leeza Gibbons Show,* the *Maury Povich Show, Star Trek: Voyager, South of Sunset, JAG, Sabrina the Teenage Witch,* and several movies of the week. Warner Television was also among my first clients, and several people there went the extra mile for me by encouraging their shows to use my material.

After the initial success of my company, I decided to take things to the next level. I determined that if I was going to be competitive with the other music providers in the industry, I needed to have a better presentation than the cassettes and DAT tapes (digital audiotapes) that I had been using. I decided to produce a collection of CDs, as this medium was industry standard. I signed sixty-five different writers to my company and compiled nearly 120 different songs in a dozen different genres. I knew this was going to be a huge financial (and emotional) investment for me, but I felt it was something I needed to do. Up to this point, I had kinda just stuck my foot in the water with music publishing; now I decided to jump in headfirst! I invested nearly $30,000 and six months in this project. I was nervous about it, but it turned out to be the best investment I could have ever made. The CDs made it easier for people to hear my material, and the catalog became even more user-friendly than before. In the first six months after I'd sent them out, I recouped my investment twofold, and my beer money became my career money!

I went on to license over two hundred songs in the first twelve months I had my CDs, including songs in *ER, Melrose Place, Mad About You, Beverly Hills 90210, Promised Land,*

Touched by an Angel, General Hospital, Friends, Lois and Clark, Sisters, X-Files, Millennium, Chicago Hope, Buffy the Vampire Slayer, and numerous made-for-TV movies. To top it off, I had ten different songs used for the 1996 Summer Olympics and was awarded a special commendation for musical contributions to the Emmy Award–winning daytime soap opera *Guiding Light.*

Recently, I finished compiling my sixth volume of CDs, this one comprising twenty-two CDs' worth of music. I am also expanding beyond film and TV to provide music for commercials, Web sites, corporate presentations, video games, network promos, movie trailers, and in-house productions. There is a huge market for music that I have just begun to tap into. I'm learning as I'm going, and that's half the fun of it. It's been said that hard work has its rewards, and I am certainly seeing the fruits of my labor blossom. When I started my business, I had no idea that it would develop into what it is today. I feel very fortunate that I was able to carve out a little niche for myself in this field. I firmly believe that *everybody* has the ability to find his own little niche, whatever it is. You may not find that thing right away (I didn't), but eventually everything always seems to work out okay in the end. Being your own boss certainly has its advantages, but on the flip side, it's a huge responsibility. Still, I don't think I would want to work for anyone else if I didn't have to.

ODD JOBS

I've had a variety of jobs throughout the years. Some were more conducive to a musician's lifestyle than others. Earlier, I mentioned that when I first moved to Boston, I bussed tables and washed dishes at a restaurant. I also worked at a clothing sweatshop ironing seams, and made macramé pots for an interior decorating company. All these jobs involved long, tedious hours and were physically (and emotionally) draining. I'd come back from a ten-hour day and just be *exhausted.* It was tough to summon up the energy to go rehearse for another four or five hours and start all over again the next day. One day, I saw an ad in the paper from the paper itself: the publication was looking for telephone solicitors to bolster its subscription department. The hours were pretty flexible and offered a competitive hourly salary plus commission. I had never tried phone sales before, but I had a friend who did pretty well at it, so I gave it a try. I wound up making almost twice as much as I had made with my previous jobs! I hadn't realized I had the gift of gab before that time, but I was glad I found out that I did. I wound up staying in telephone sales the rest of my time in Massachusetts, supplementing my teaching income. When I moved out to California, I continued in telephone sales, eventually finding work at an advertising agency that sold ad space for various magazines. I wound up staying there on and off for eight years, coming back in between tours, and leaving again whenever the road beckoned. Telephone sales seems to be a perfect choice for musicians; you don't need any prior experience in the field to try it, you can look like whatever you want to, you don't have to operate any dangerous machinery that may endanger your body, and you can usually find hours that are agreeable to your lifestyle. You also may find yourself pleasantly surprised at the amount of money you can make at a sales position. I know people who have made $45,000 per year working part-time hours!

CHAPTER 9

*Stayin' Sane—Help Is on the Way:
Chemical and Alcohol Dependency*

It is a sad, unfortunate fact that there are some people who
succumb to the excesses of the rock 'n' roll lifestyle. Although
there are substance abuse casualties in all walks of life, the
entertainment industry seems particularly vulnerable. The
smoke screens of fame, fortune, and adulation often hide lonely
people who turn to drugs and alcohol as escape mechanisms to
dull emotional pain. There is a difference between recreational
use and compulsive use, although the line between the two is
often blurred. There are some artists who feel that certain
drugs or alcohol stimulate their creativity, and they can't find
the creative muse without it. Although I may not personally
agree with that perspective, it is not up to me to say what
works for someone else.

I am not an expert in the fields of clinical psychology or
human behavior. Nor do I claim to know the reasons *why* people abuse drugs and alcohol. Therefore, it is not my intention to
pontificate on the issue of substance abuse, make judgments on
other people's lives, or even offer opinions on this topic. What I
do know is that way too many gifted artists have had their
careers, and even their lives, destroyed by drug and alcohol
problems. Now, I realize that some artists may have inherent
psychological or emotional problems that tend to *lead* to substance abuse, but the whole issue of chemical dependency is
extremely complex and beyond the scope of this book. This
chapter is not meant to condone or condemn drugs and alcohol,
only to point out that they do exist rather prevalently in the

music industry, and that the choice to use drugs and alcohol (and to what degree) is a unique personal decision only *you* can make. We all start out in life with a fairly clean slate. Keeping a straight head through everything requires a lot of self-discipline, determination, and, in some cases, professional help.

I am saddened by the loss of so many talented musical artists whose lives were adversely affected by drugs and alcohol throughout the years. These artists brought millions of people a lot of joy and inspiration, and I only wish they were alive to contribute more. The following names are but a partial list of great talent who left us prematurely with a legacy of work to remember them by: West Arkeen, Tommy Bolin (Deep Purple), John Bonham (Led Zeppelin), Kurt Cobain (Nirvana), Brian Connolly (Sweet), Dawn Crosby (Fear of God), Pete Farndon (the Pretenders), Andy Gibb (the Bee Gees), Ray Gillen (Black Sabbath/Badlands), Jimi Hendrix, James Honeyman-Scott (the Pretenders), Shannon Hoon (Blind Melon), Janis Joplin, Phil Lynott (Thin Lizzy), Jonathan Melvoin (Smashing Pumpkins), Keith Moon (the Who), Jim Morrison (the Doors), Bradley Nowell (Sublime), John Panozzo (Styx), Gram Parsons, Kristen Pfaff (Hole), Elvis Presley, Mick Ronson, Bon Scott (AC/DC), Hillel Slovak (Red Hot Chili Peppers), Johnny Thunders (NY Dolls), Sid Vicious, and Andrew Wood (Mother Love Bone).

In addition, there are hundreds of *living* musicians who have had their battles with substance abuse. Many have been well-publicized, such as David Crosby (who underwent a liver transplant) and Keith Richards. Others wage their wars more privately, and, in respect to their wishes, I will not list them here.

Fortunately, there are programs that a musician can turn to in times of need. One of the most far-reaching is MusiCares, sponsored by the National Academy of Recording Arts and Sciences (NARAS), the same folks who bring you the Grammys. Formed in 1989 to address the financial, health, and human service needs of musicians, MusiCares has evolved to include an industry substance abuse program, designed to provide help for those suffering from chemical dependency. As a result of the formation of this program, a music professional who needs help (or anyone wishing to help someone who may need help) can call (800) MUSICARES. Calls will be answered by an experienced social worker who will confidentially assist and refer the caller to treatment options. Financial assistance is available to those who do not have the resources to place themselves in treatment. Financial assistance may take the form of rent, utilities, sustenance, medicine and prescriptions, substance abuse intervention and treatment, HIV and AIDS treatment, psychotherapy, and other expenses related to the above categories.

In addition, MusiCares has established industrywide committees, whose individual members will speak to the concerns of their particular segment of the music community. At press time, cochairs include the heads of MCA Records, Capitol Records, Virgin Records America, Revolution Records, and several high-profile managers and attorneys. Special fund-raising events and an industry payroll pledge program help support this wonderful cause. NARAS also makes available pamphlets and brochures that are designed to provide education about drug awareness and prevention. And remember: An ounce of prevention is worth a ton of cure.

Other programs that may be available include Alcoholics Anonymous and Al-Anon, both found in your local phone book. In addition, many local communities offer twenty-four-hour crisis hotlines, drug intervention and referral programs, and health care programs. Taking that first step and getting help is the best thing you can do for yourself and the ones who love you.

EPILOGUE

It is my sincere wish that this book has been helpful to you. More than anything, I wanted this to be a beacon of light to those who may have felt like they were in the dark. Many times during the course of my career, I could have used a little light at the end of the tunnel. Your path to success may be different than mine, but, ultimately, the journey goes through similar terrain.

I am reminded of a saying that has stuck in my head ever since I can remember. What I *can't* remember, however, is where I heard it first. I may have read it somewhere, or perhaps heard it in conversation. I may have even thought of it myself, but if it has been attributed to someone else, I extend my humble apologies to the author. This motto is one that I have always lived my life by. Perhaps it can do for you what it has done for me. It goes like this:

Follow your dreams . . . and someday,
your dreams will follow you.

Best wishes on the follow-through.

GLOSSARY

ADMINISTRATION DEAL: Business arrangement where a person or company will provide copyright, accounting, and royalty services for your song catalog without having an ownership in the compositions.

A&R: Artist and repertoire. The A&R person at a record company is responsible for finding and signing new talent and acting as the band's general contact at the label.

BIDDING WAR: Situation where several record companies may be interested in the same artist, therefore driving up the price for the artist's contract.

CONTROLLED COMPOSITION CLAUSE: Provision in a record contract that allows the record company to reduce the statutory mechanical rate it pays to the artist on the songs that the artist controls.

CUT: Music industry term for the use of a song covered on someone's album.

DEMO DEAL: Arrangement in which a record company pays for the recording of a tape to hear a sample of an artist's material without committing to a full record contract. The record company would normally have the first right to sign the artist.

ENGINEER: Person who assists in the physical aspects of the recording process, such as wiring the studio, setting up the equipment and running the tape machines. The assistants to engineers are called "seconds."

FANZINES: Publications written by fans.

IN-HOUSE: Done from within a company, instead of hiring outside vendors. Usually pertains to a record company's promotion or publicity department.

KEY MAN CLAUSE: Provision that may allow artists to get out of their record contract if certain specified people leave the record company.

LEAVING MEMBER CLAUSE: Provision in a record contract that allows the record company to retain the exclusive recording services of a band member should he leave the group or the group disband.

LICENSEE: One who licenses something from the owner of a specific property. In the field of film and TV the licensee may typically be a TV show or a movie company.

LICENSOR: One who licenses something to a second party.

MECHANICAL INCOME: Income generated by the mechanical reproduction of songs on an album. Paid to the writers and publishers by the record companies at a set rate, known as the statutory mechanical rate.

NEEDLEDROP: Term describing a very short use of a song in a film or TV show, normally five seconds or less in duration.

PARTNERSHIP AGREEMENT: A contractual arrangement drawn up between members of a band that defines the legal and business relationship of the group.

PER DIEM: A Latin term meaning "each day." Refers to amount of money an artist receives each day while on the road to cover normal everyday expenses.

PERFORMANCE CLAUSE: Provision that states that certain goals (usually financial) are met in order for a contract to continue. Normally found in artist/manager agreements.

PERFORMANCE INCOME: Income paid to the publishers and writers of music that has been played in a public place, on radio or television. These monies are paid by the performing rights organizations.

PERFORMING RIGHTS ORGANIZATIONS: Organizations that monitor the public performances of music and, in turn, pay royalties to their publisher and writer affiliates. The three biggest performance rights societies in the United States are ASCAP, BMI, and SESAC.

POINT: Monetary amount equivalent to 1 percent of the retail selling price of a product such as a record, tape, compact disc, or video.

PREPRODUCTION: Rehearsal time before a band enters the studio. Arrangements and song selection are worked out with the producer before the start of recording.

PRODUCTION DEAL: Legal arrangement in which an artist signs an agreement with a producer or production company whereby that entity enters into a recording contract with a label. Hence, the artist is not signed directly to the label.

RECOUPABLE: Any item that may be charged back to the artist, such as recording budgets, video budgets, tour support or certain promotional expenditures.

RETAINER: Monetary figure that an attorney may require from a client to start or keep his services.

RIDER: Agreement an artist has with the concert promoter that provides items such as food, beverages, sundries, or other miscellaneous items.

SHOP: Term describing the process of sending tapes to a record company for consideration ("shopping" a tape).

SPEC TIME: Short for *speculative,* this is recording time that a studio may allow an artist to make a demo tape. The studio may ask for remuneration at some point, perhaps if the tape is instrumental in getting the artist a record contract.

STATUTORY MECHANICAL RATE: Monetary amount record companies must pay to the writers and publishers of each song on a record, paid on each copy sold. Current rate is eight cents.

SYNCHRONIZATION FEE: Fee negotiated for the use of a song in a production, such as a movie or TV show, allowing the song to be synchronized with the picture.

TAKE: Term for the amount of money that may be earned on a given night's performance. Applies to box office gross receipts and merchandising receipts.

VIDEOGRAM BUYOUT: Fee negotiated for the right to include a song in a video for sale.

BIBLIOGRAPHY

All You Need to Know About the Music Business
Donald S. Passman
Simon & Schuster Trade, 1997
ISBN#: 0684836009

Breaking into the Music Business
Alan H. Siegel
Simon & Schuster Trade, 1991
ISBN#: 0671729071

The Craft & Business of Songwriting
John Braheny
F & W Publications Inc., 1995
ISBN#: 0898796539

Hit Men: Power Brokers & Fast Money Inside the Music Business
Fredric Dannen
Random House, Inc., 1991
ISBN#: 0679730613

Home Recording for Musicians, rev. ed.
Craig Anderton
Music Sales Corporation, 1996
ISBN#: 0825615003

Making It in the Music Business: A Business & Legal Guide for Songwriters & Performers
Lee Wilson
Allworth Press, 1999
ISBN#: 1581150369

Making Music Your Business
David Ellefson
Miller Freeman, Inc.
(Book Division), 1997
ISBN#: 087930460X

The Mansion on the Hill: Dylan, Young, Geffen, Springsteen and the Head-On Collision of Rock and Commerce
Fred Goodman
Random House, Inc., 1997
ISBN#: 0812921135

Money in Music: Everything a Musician Needs to Know to Become Steadily Employed as a Live Performer
Craig Warren Colley
Houston Publishing, Inc., 1997
ISBN#: 1565160002

Music Business: Career Opportunities and Self-Defense, rev. updated ed.
Dick Weissman
Crown Publishing Group, 1990
ISBN#: 0517575248

The Music Business (Explained in Plain English): What Every Artist & Songwriter Should Know to Avoid Getting Ripped Off!
David Nagger and Jeffrey D. Brandstetter
Daje Publishing, 1996
ISBN#: 0964870908

Music Business Handbook & Career Guide
David Baskerville
Sage Publications, Inc., 1995
ISBN#: 0803971532

The Musician's Business and
Legal Guide, 2d ed.
Mark Halloran
Prentice Hall, 1996
ISBN#: 013237322X

Music, Money, & Success: The Insider's
Guide to the Music Industry
Jeffrey Brabec and Todd Brabec
Schirmer Books, 1994
ISBN#: 002870133X

Music Publishing: A Songwriter's
Guide, rev. ed.
Randy Poe
Writers Digest Books, 2001
ISBN#: 0898797543

National Directory of Record Labels
& Music Publishers
Barbara Taylor and
Michael Peterson, eds.
Rising Star Music Publishers,
1995
ISBN#: 0963442171

The Rock File: Making It
in the Music Business
Norton York, editor
Oxford University Press, Inc., 1992
ISBN#: 0198162480

Rough Mix: An Unapologetic Look at
the Music Business and How It Got
That Way—A Lifetime in the World of
Rock, Pop, and Country, as Told by One
of the Industry's Most Powerful Players
Jimmy Bowen
Simon & Schuster Trade, 1997
ISBN#: 0684807645

Running Your Own
Rock & Roll Band
William Henderson
Macmillan Publishing Company,
Inc., 1996
ISBN#: 0028646118

The Songwriter's Rhyming Dictionary
Jane Shaw Whitfield
Wilshire Book Company, 1975
ISBN#: 0879802936

This Business of Music, 7th ed.
M. William Krasilovsky and
Sidney Shemel
Watson-Guptill Publications, Inc.,
1995
ISBN#: 0823077551

Writing Music for Hit Songs:
Including Songs From the '90s
Jai Josefs
Schirmer Books, 1996
ISBN#: 0028646789

JOURNALS, NEWSLETTERS, PAMPHLETS, AND OTHER RESOURCES

A&R 411
c/o SRS Publishing
7510 Sunset Boulevard, Suite 1041
Los Angeles, CA 90046-3418
(818) 769-2722
(800) 377-7411
A comprehensive guide listing A&R
staff, their direct phone and fax
numbers, and assistants' names.
Includes major and independent
labels. Updated regularly.

Hollywood Blu-Book
5055 Wilshire Boulevard, Suite 600
Los Angeles, CA 90036
(323) 525-2000
Published by the *Hollywood*
Reporter, this is a virtual "yellow
pages" for the entertainment industry. Includes an A to Z listing of
individuals and organizations in
film, television, music, and related
services.

Hollywood Creative Directory
3000 Olympic Boulevard, Suite 2413
Santa Monica, CA 90404
(310) 315-4815
Provides contact information and
brief credit histories for major
studios and film and television
production companies.

Hollywood Reporter
5055 Wilshire Boulevard
Los Angeles, CA 90036
(323) 525-2000
Covers news regarding U.S. and
international developments in the
entertainment industry. Often prints
special supplements on events or
topics of special interest, including
periodic features on film and television music. The Tuesday edition
features a list of film and television
projects currently in production.
Published daily.

Variety
5700 Wilshire Boulevard, Suite 120
Los Angeles, CA 90030
(323) 857-6600
A prominent national trade publication that emphasizes films and
television productions. The Friday
edition features film and television
projects currently in production.
Published daily.

*Motion Picture, TV and
Theatre Directory*
Herbert R. Pilzer
New York: Motion Picture
Enterprises Publications, Inc.
This semiannual directory has a
comprehensive index of production
services and offers information
about a wide variety of resources.

RESOURCES

PERFORMING RIGHTS ORGANIZATIONS

ASCAP—New York
1 Lincoln Plaza
New York, NY 10023
(212) 621-6000
(800) 952-7227

ASCAP—Los Angeles
7920 Sunset Boulevard, 3rd Floor
Los Angeles, CA 90046
(323) 883-1000

ASCAP—Nashville
2 Music Square West
Nashville, TN 37203
(615) 742-5000

BMI—New York
320 West 57th Street
New York, NY 10019
(212) 586-2000

BMI—Los Angeles
8730 Sunset Boulevard
3rd Floor West
Los Angeles, CA 90069
(310) 659-9109

BMI—Nashville
10 Music Square East
Nashville, TN 37203
(615) 401-2000

SESAC—New York
421 West 54th Street, 4th Floor
New York, NY 10019
(212) 586-3450

SESAC—Los Angeles
501 Santa Monica Boulevard
Suite 450
Santa Monica, CA 90401
(310) 393-9671

SESAC—Nashville
55 Music Square West
Nashville, TN 37203
(615) 320-0055
(800) 826-9996

SONGWRITER ORGANIZATIONS

Nashville Songwriters Association
International
15 Music Square West
Nashville, TN 37203

National Academy of Songwriters
6255 Sunset Boulevard
Suite 1023
Hollywood, CA 90028
(323) 463-7178

Songwriters Guild of America
6430 Sunset Boulevard
Suite 317
Hollywood, CA 90028
(323) 462-1108

Society of Composers
and Lyricists
400 South Beverly Drive
Suite 214
Beverly Hills, CA 90212
(310) 281-2812

PUBLISHER ORGANIZATIONS
Association of Independent
Music Publishers
P.O. Box 1561
Burbank, CA 91507
(818) 842-6257

California Copyright Conference
P.O. Box 1291
Burbank, CA 91507
(818) 848-6783

Harry Fox Agency
205 East 42nd Street
New York, NY 10017
(212) 370-5330

PROFESSIONAL ORGANIZATIONS
Academy of Motion Picture Arts
and Sciences (AMPAS)
8949 Wilshire Boulevard
Beverly Hills, CA 90211
(310) 247-3000

American Federation of Musicians
(AFM)—Hollywood
Professional Musicians Local 47
817 Vine Street
Hollywood, CA 90038
(323) 462-2161

American Federation of
Musicians—New York
Paramount Building
1501 Broadway, Suite 600
New York, NY 10036
(212) 869-1330
(800) 762-3444

American Federation of Television
and Radio Artists (AFTRA)—
New York
260 Madison Avenue
7th Floor
New York, NY 10016
(212) 532-0800

American Federation of Television
and Radio Artists (AFTRA)—
Los Angeles
5757 Wilshire Boulevard
9th Floor
Los Angeles, CA 90036
(323) 634-8100

Los Angeles Music Network
P.O. Box 8934
Universal City, CA 91618-8934
(818) 769-6095

Motion Picture Association of
America (MPAA)
15503 Ventura Boulevard
Encino, CA 91436
(818) 995-6600

National Academy of Recording
Arts and Sciences (NARAS)
3402 Pico Boulevard
Santa Monica, CA 90405
(310) 392-3777

National Academy of Television
Arts and Sciences (NATAS)—
New York
110 West 57th Street
Suite 1020
New York, NY 10019
(212) 586-8424

National Academy of Television
Arts and Sciences (NATAS)—
Los Angeles
5220 Lankershim Boulevard
North Hollywood, CA 91601
(818) 754-2800

INDEX

BOOKS FROM ALLWORTH PRESS

How to Pitch and Promote Your Songs by Fred Koller (paperback, 6 × 9, 208 pages, $19.95)

The Art of Writing Great Lyrics by Pamela Phillips Oland (paperback, 6 × 9, 256 pages, $18.95)

Profiting from Your Music and Sound Project Studio by Jeffrey P. Fisher (paperback, 6 × 9, 274 pages, $18.95)

Moving Up in the Music Business by Jodi Summers (paperback, 6 × 9, 224 pages, $18.95)

The Songwriter's and Musician's Guide to Nashville, Revised Edition by Sherry Bond (paperback, 6 × 9, 256 pages, $18.95)

Creative Careers in Music by Josquin des Pres and Mark Landsman (paperback, 6 × 9, 224 pages, $18.95)

Making It in the Music Business: The Business and Legal Guide for Songwriters and Performers, Revised Edition by Lee Wilson (paperback, 6 × 9, 288 pages, $18.95)

Making and Marketing Music: The Musician's Guide to Financing, Distributing, and Promoting Albums by Jodi Summers (paperback, 6 × 9, 240 pages, $18.95)

Booking and Tour Management for the Performing Arts, Revised Edition by Rena Shagan (paperback, 6 × 9, 276 pages, $19.95)

Career Solutions for Creative People by Dr. Ronda Ormont (paperback, 306 pages, 6 × 9, $19.95)

The Interactive Music Handbook: The Definitive Guide to Internet Music Strategies, Enhanced CD Production, and Business Development by Jodi Summers (paperback, 6 × 9, 296 pages, $18.95)

The Copyright Guide: A Friendly Guide to Protecting and Profiting from Copyrights, Revised Edition by Lee Wilson (paperback, 6 × 9, 208 pages, $19.95)

The Trademark Guide: A Friendly Guide to Protecting and Profiting from Trademarks by Lee Wilson (paperback, 6 × 9, 208 pages, $18.95)

Artists Communities: A Directory of Residencies in the United States That Offer Time and Space for Creativity, Second Edition by the Alliance of Artists' Communities (paperback, 6¾ × 10, 256 pages, $18.95)

Please write to request our free catalog. To order by credit card, call 1-800-491-2808 or send a check or money order to Allworth Press, 10 East 23rd Street, Suite 510, New York, NY 10010. Include $5 for shipping and handling for the first book ordered and $1 for each additional book. Ten dollars plus $1 for each additional book if ordering from Canada. New York State residents must add sales tax.

To see our complete catalog on the World Wide Web, or to order online, you can find us at *www.allworth.com*.